AF686022

Declarative Mapping Sentences in Qualitative Research

In this book, Hackett introduces the traditional usage of the mapping sentence within quantitative research, reviews its philosophical underpinnings, and proposes the "declarative mapping sentence" as an instrument and approach to qualitative scholarship.

With a helpful glossary and a range of illustrative tables, Hackett takes the reader through a straightforward introduction to mapping sentences and their construction, before discussing declarative mapping sentences and possible future research directions. This innovative direction for social research provides a flexible structure for research domain, and it allows qualitative research results to be uniformly sorted.

Declarative Mapping Sentences in Qualitative Research will be essential reading for researchers, academics, and postgraduate students in the fields of qualitative psychology and psychological methods, as well as philosophical psychology and social science research methods.

Paul M. W. Hackett is a professor of ethnography and research methods at Emerson College, U.S.A. He is also a visiting professor in health research methods at the University of Suffolk and visiting scholar at the Royal Anthropological Institute, London, UK.

Routledge Research in Psychology

This series offers an international forum for original and innovative research being conducted across the field of psychology. Titles in the series are empirically or theoretically informed and explore a range of dynamic and timely issues and emerging topics. The series is aimed at upper-level and post-graduate students, researchers, and research students, as well as academics and scholars.

Recent titles in the series include:

Declarative Mapping Sentences in Qualitative Research
Theoretical, Linguistic, and Applied Usages
Paul M. W. Hackett

For a complete list of titles in this series, please visit: www.routledge.com

Declarative Mapping Sentences in Qualitative Research

Theoretical, Linguistic, and Applied Usages

Paul M. W. Hackett

Routledge
Taylor & Francis Group
NEW YORK AND LONDON

First published 2021
by Routledge
52 Vanderbilt Avenue, New York, NY 10017

and by Routledge
2 Park Square, Milton Park, Abingdon, Oxon, OX14 4RN

Routledge is an imprint of the Taylor & Francis Group, an informa business

© 2021 Taylor & Francis

The right of Paul M. W. Hackett to be identified as author of this work has been asserted by him in accordance with sections 77 and 78 of the Copyright, Designs and Patents Act 1988.

All rights reserved. No part of this book may be reprinted or reproduced or utilised in any form or by any electronic, mechanical, or other means, now known or hereafter invented, including photocopying and recording, or in any information storage or retrieval system, without permission in writing from the publishers.

Trademark notice: Product or corporate names may be trademarks or registered trademarks, and are used only for identification and explanation without intent to infringe.

Library of Congress Cataloging-in-Publication Data
A catalog record for this book has been requested

ISBN: 978-1-138-49982-9 (hbk)
ISBN: 978-1-351-01399-4 (ebk)

Typeset in Times New Roman
by Apex CoVantage, LLC

To Jessica and Malmesbury

Contents

Other books on facet theory and mapping sentences by Paul M. W. Hackett include

Hackett, P.M.W. (2020) **The Complexity of Bird Behaviour: A Facet Theory Approach,** Cham, CH: Springer.

Hackett, P.M.W. and Fisher, Y. (eds.) (2019) **Advances in Facet Theory Research: Developments in Theory and Application and Competing Approaches,** Lausanne, Switzerland: Frontiers Media SA

Hackett, P.M.W. (ed.) (2019) **Conceptual Categories and the Structure of Reality: Theoretical and Empirical Approaches**, Lausanne, Switzerland: Frontiers Media SA

Hackett, P.M.W. (ed.) (2018) **Mereologies, Ontologies and Facets: The Categorial Structure of Reality,** Lanham, MD: Lexington

Hackett, P.M.W. (2017) **The Perceptual Structure of Three-Dimensional Art,** Heidelberg: Springer

Hackett, P.M.W. (2016) **Psychology and Philosophy of Abstract Art: Neuro-aesthetics, Perception and Comprehension,** Basingstoke: Palgrave.

Hackett, P.M.W. (2014) **Facet Theory and the Mapping Sentence: Evolving Philosophy, Use and Application**, Basingstoke: Palgrave.

Hackett, P.M.W. (2013) **Fine Art and Perceptual Neuroscience: Field of Vision and the Painted Grid, Explorations in Cognitive Psychology Series,** London: Psychology Press.

Hackett, P.M.W. (1995) **Conservation and the Consumer: Understanding Environmental Concern**. London: Routledge Publishers

Acknowledgements

There are many individuals who have played an important role in the research upon which this book is based. Emeritus Professor David Canter from Huddersfield University was the first to instil in me a belief and interest in facet theory. My life has not been the same since I read his 1985 book, *Facet Theory: Approaches to Social Research*. Thank you, David.

As well as those who have added to the overall development of my research in the area of facet theory and the mapping sentence, there are several people I would like to thank for their more direct influence on the writing in this book. I would first like to thank Professor Anna Marmodoro, who holds the E. J. Lowe Chair in Metaphysics in the Department of Philosophy at Durham University, for hosting me as an honorary fellow in the philosophy department.

Figures and Tables

Figures

Tables

Preface

This book is aimed at two groups of readers. The first group comprises researchers and scholars who are familiar with the traditional facet theory approach to quantitative social research but have not as yet encountered qualitative facet theory or the declarative mapping sentence. The second group is made up of scholars and researchers who are new to any form of facet-theory-driven research and any use of the mapping sentence in social and behavioural inquiries. As the book is aimed at these two reader groups, I will provide basic details of the facet theory approach, but I will not go into great detail about the theory. I guide readers interested in learning more about the approach to the additional reading section at the end of the preface.

Facet theory research has foundations in the notion that behaviours, psychological processes, and other such phenomena are experienced categorially (Hackett, 2018, 2019a). When a researcher embodies a research orientation that embraces a facet theory perspective, he or she will also adopt a specific philosophical view or orientation towards the human animals in their investigations (Hackett, 2014).[1] Fundamentally, the facet theory perspective to research attempts to develop knowledge regarding the behaviours and experiences that are of interest to the scholar, based upon the understanding that these phenomena are made up of categorial components. Contingent upon such an understanding are notions that by breaking-down research areas into their sub-components, researchers believe that they will place themselves in a better position to investigate the area that is the focus of the research. When using a facet theory approach, having broken-down a research area into its essential sub-elements, information is then gathered that is representative of the specified sub-components. However, crucially within facet, research is conducted that investigates the sub-components of a research domain as the sub-components exist as a phenomenological whole. During the analysis stages of the research, the separately identified components, known as facets and facet elements, are evaluated as they interact in the usual setting of their occurrence, in order to provide a greater understanding of their combined relationships to the totality of the research area.

Louis Guttman developed facet theory as a phenomenological and systemic approach to behavioural science research (Guttman, 1947, 1959). His methodology explicitly divided up an area of research interest into a categorial classification system in a systematic and explicit way by using what he called a mapping sentence (see Shye et al., 1994, pp. 70–95). His research yielded data that were numerical and subject to empirical testing (see, Canter, 1985; Shye, 1978; Shye et al., 1974; Borg and Shye, 1995). In this book, I call Guttman's approach to facet theory and the use of the mapping sentence "traditional facet theory" or "quantitative facet theory" and the type of mapping sentence he used in his research the "traditional mapping sentence". In his highly influential writing about facet theory as an approach to research in the social sciences, David Canter (1985) emphasises how important the mapping sentence is in facet theory research when he claims that "a piece of facet research is a process of refinement, elaboration and validation of a mapping sentence" (p 266).

Indeed, within facet theory, the mapping sentence is the main research tool and constitutes the basic fabric of the approach. Within the pages of this book, it is my aim to initially introduce and then to consolidate understanding of the mapping sentence as it has been used both in quantitative research design and as a quantitative analysis technique. Therefore, I will commence by introducing the traditional usage of the mapping sentence within quantitative research. However, my research and writing will go far beyond the usual quantitative application of mapping sentences. The title of the present book incorporates the phrase *declarative mapping sentences*. Declarative mapping sentences are a sub-type of mapping sentences that are used in qualitative, theoretical, and philosophical inquiries. As well as presenting traditional mapping sentence usage, I will review the philosophical underpinnings of the mapping sentence, consider its linguistic foundations, and propose the declarative mapping sentence as an instrument and approach to scholarship in qualitative, narrative-based, or more philosophical forms of research. I will also make reference to my use of the mapping sentence as a tool in counselling and therapy (Hackett, 2019c).

There are several books that take traditional facet theory as their subject matter. There are two texts, one by Canter (1985) and the other by Shye and Elizur (1994) that may be argued as being the basis of popular facet theory. As well as these two texts, there are also many statistically based books and other types of publications on the subject (for example, Borg and Lingoes, 1987; Borg et al., 2018). The book by Shye and Elizur (1994) is perhaps the most widely read and also the most commonly used text in teaching facet theory. Both this and Canter's (1995) book are excellent, and the book of readings by David Canter (1985) provides a comprehensive and authoritative introduction both to facet theory itself and to the many substantive research areas in which facet theory has been used as a guide to designing and analysing a wide variety of investigations. The mapping sentence is addressed in the aforementioned books but in a slightly instrumental sense. By this, I mean that the mapping sentence is considered a tool for use by researchers and as a device that is used in quantitative facet theory research. Both of the preceding books, and indeed all of the other texts on facet theory (with the exception of some of my own writing), are different from the present book in that they do not consider the mapping sentence in the following senses:

- as a stand-alone instrument for use in research and scholarship
- as a philosophical device
- as a qualitative research instrument
- in terms of the linguistic-semantic structure of the mapping sentence

The books by Canter (1985) and Shye and Elizur (1994) complement the present text, which concentrates on the preceding four aspects of mapping sentences along with the use of the mapping sentence in social and other forms of research that is *non-numerical*. The present book also provides a chapter on how to develop a mapping sentence.

My Writing on Qualitative Facet Theory and the Declarative Mapping Sentence

I first started to conduct facet theory research around 35 years ago (Hackett, 1985). During this time, I have thought about facet theory from many perspectives and have employed the approach within many types and areas of research. However, over the last decade, I have mainly focussed my attention on the use of the facet theory within qualitative research, as an approach to philosophical scholarship and upon the philosophical and linguistic considerations of facet theory. In my book from the last decade (Hackett, 2014), I reviewed the mapping sentence as it has been used over the last 70 plus years within quantitative facet theory research. In this previous book and in subsequent writing, I went on to propose extensions and modifications to the mapping sentence and to its usage within non-quantitative research settings. This new book constitutes the culmination of a transitional phase in my facet theory and mapping sentence research. In Hackett (2014), I made suggestions that mapping sentences could and should be used to design and analyse non-numerical data, including such information types as narratives and *rich* observational data. I also, perhaps more contentiously, suggested that a mapping sentence need not have an explicit range facet. My 2014 text also presented details about how I had, in my work, been using the mapping sentence both to guide my own fine art painting and to investigate the philosophy of fine art.[2] I explored the experience of different forms of abstract art (Hackett, 2016, 2017a), and I used mapping sentences to explore visual impairment (2013) and as a form of counselling therapy (Hackett, 2019c).

A major part of my research into non-numerical facet theory has involved the development of a specific type of mapping sentence for use in a non-quantitative context which, as I have already noted, I have called the declarative mapping sentence to distinguish it from the traditional mapping sentence and to emphasise the fact that the sentence constitutes a declaration in regard to the experiential structure of a phenomenon or a research domain (Hackett, 2018, 2019b). Taken together, my two books (Hackett, 2016, 2017a) embody my use of the declarative mapping sentence to design research into abstract fine art of different media and dimensional formats. The two books use the mapping sentence in an applied qualitative/philosophical context.

The present book further considers the theoretical underpinnings of the declarative mapping sentence and how and when the declarative mapping sentence may be used. This present book is the first to present the traditional mapping sentence alongside the declarative mapping sentence. Within its pages, I discuss traditional, declarative, and philosophical aspects of these mapping sentences and how to use these with concentration placed upon the declarative mapping sentence. As I noted earlier, with the exception of my own research, the mapping sentence has almost exclusively been employed within quantitative facet theory research. This book is unique in the literature in that it views the mapping sentence as a theoretical, linguistic, and applied research device that is independent from other theoretical orientations, including those that are encompassed within the facet theory approach.

Researchers engage in many types of reasoning during their professional activities in attempts to clarify their thoughts and feelings, and they frequently return to and re-explore their research and its findings (Walton, 2001). The present book proposes the declarative mapping sentence as embodying a philosophical orientation as well as being a qualitative research tool. Throughout the book, I will attempt to provide substance to my claim that the declarative mapping sentence can guide research and scholarship in qualitative and narrative-based research and provide a flexible template for re-exploring and clarifying a researcher's findings.

Synopsis of Chapters

Chapter 1 – Introduction to Mapping Sentences

In this first chapter, I provide brief details about facet theory and the mapping sentence as this has been traditionally used. In order to clearly describe and explain mapping sentences, I will include examples of mapping sentences found in, using mapping sentences within a qualitative and philosophical research context.

Chapter 2 – Constructing a Mapping Sentence

Having introduced mapping sentences in the first chapter, and before I proceed to discuss mapping sentences in greater detail in Chapter 3, in the second chapter, I provide a hands-on description of how a mapping sentence is actually produced. I make this as easy to understand as possible by using a single research domain as an example. As is typical in research that uses a mapping sentence, the research domain in this example is complex and is composed of multiple interconnected variables. I commence the illustration of how to design and develop a mapping sentence with simple single independent and dependant variables. From this, I make the design increasingly more complicated by including the simultaneous effects of an increasing number of variables. I also comment upon the usefulness of developing a mapping sentence as a standardised research framework and how this can yield cumulative findings, consistency in the interpretations of the data, and knowledge development.

Chapter 3 – Declarative Mapping Sentences

This chapter will provide particulars about my claims for the need for the mapping sentence in qualitative and philosophical scholarship. I note how the declarative nature of this mapping sentence instrument may be traced to its linguistic sources, and I give examples of declarative mapping sentences from my own research, which has focussed upon issues in the social sciences and humanities. I make the argument for the utility of a sentence as being suitable for structuring complex research that is clearly defined and bounded by a framework provided by the sentence's linguistic components.

Chapter 4 – Conclusion and Future Research

In the final chapter, I will provide suggestions regarding the direction in which mapping sentence and declarative mapping sentence research may be taken in the future. The suggestions that I make in this chapter will be based on both my ongoing research in this area and the research of others.

Further Reading

Canter, D. (ed.) (1985) *Facet Theory: Approaches to Social Research*, New York: Springer Verlag (there is also a 2011 reprint).

Clark, M. (2015) Facet Theory: An Analytical Approach for Research Design, in Bezzina, F., and Cassar, V. (eds.) *Ecrm 2015 – Proceedings of the 14th European Conference on Research Methodology for Business and Management Studies*, Sonning Common: Academic Conferences Publishing Limited.

Dancer, L. (1990) Introduction to Facet Theory and Its Applications, *Applied Psychology*, 39(4), 365–377.

Hackett, P.M.W., and Fisher, Y. (eds.) (2019) *Advances in Facet Theory Research: Developments in Theory and Application and Competing Approaches*, Lausanne, Switzerland: Frontiers Media SA.

References

Borg, I., Groenen, P.J.F., and Mair, P. (2018) *Applied Multidimensional Scaling and Unfolding* (Springer Briefs in Statistics), New York: Springer.

Borg, I., and Lingoes, J. (1987) *Multidimensional Similarity Structure Analysis*, New York: Springer.

Canter, D. (ed.) (1985) *Facet Theory: Approaches to Social Research* (Springer Series in Social Psychology), New York: Springer Verlag.

Crowther, P. (2007) *Defining Art, Creating the Canon: Artistic Value in an Era of Doubt*, Oxford: Oxford University Press.

Guttman, L. (1947) Scale and Intensity Analysis for Attitude, Opinion and Achievement, in Kelly, G.A. (ed.) *New Methods in Applied Psychology: Proceedings of the Maryland Conference on Military Contributions to Methodology in Applied Psychology Held at the University of Maryland, November 27–28, 1945, Under the Auspices of the Military Division of the American Psychological Association*, College Park, MD: University of Maryland.

Guttman, L. (1959) Introduction to Facet Design and Analysis, in *Proceedings of the Fifteenth International Congress of Psychology*, Amsterdam: North Holland, 130–132.

Hackett, P.M.W. (1983) Observations on Blink Rates in Ferruginous Duck (Aythya Nyroca) in a Flock of Mainly Mallard (Anas Platyrhynchos), Working Paper/ Field Notes.

Hackett, P.M.W. (1985) *Birmingham International Airport User Evaluation Study: A Facet Appraisal*, Unpublished Undergraduate Dissertation, Applied Psychology Department, University of Aston in Birmingham.

Hackett, P.M.W. (2014) *Facet Theory and the Mapping Sentence: Evolving Philosophy, Use and Application*, Basingstoke: Palgrave.

Hackett, P.M.W. (2016) *Psychology and Philosophy of Abstract Art: Neuro-aesthetics, Perception and Comprehension*, Basingstoke: Palgrave.

Hackett, P.M.W. (2017a) *The Perceptual Structure of Three-Dimensional Art* (Springer Briefs in Philosophy), Cham, CH: Springer.

Hackett, P.M.W. (2017b) Commentary: Wild Psychometrics: Evidence for 'General' Cognitive Performance in Wild New Zealand Robins, Petroica Longipes, *Frontiers in Psychology, Section Theoretical and Philosophical Psychology*, 8, 165. https://doi.org/10.3389/fpsyg.2017.00165.

Hackett, P.M.W. (2018) Declarative Mapping Sentence Mereologies: Categories from Aristotle to Lowe, in Hackett, P.M.W. (ed.) *Mereologies, Ontologies and Facets: The Categorial Structure of Reality*, Lanham, MD: Lexington, 135–159.

Hackett, P.M.W. (ed.) (2019a) *Conceptual Categories and the Structure of Reality: Theoretical and Empirical Approaches*, Lausanne, Switzerland: Frontiers Media SA.

Hackett, P.M.W. (2019b) Declarative Mapping Sentences as a Co-ordinating Framework for Qualitative Health and Wellbeing Research, *Journal of Social Science & Allied Health Professions*, 2(1), E1–E6.

Hackett, P.M.W. (2019c) Facet Mapping Therapy: The Potential of a Facet Theoretical Philosophy and Declarative Mapping Sentences within a Therapeutic Setting, *Frontiers in Psychology, Section Psychology for Clinical Settings*. https://doi.org/10.3389/fpsyg.2019.0122.

Hackett, P.M.W. (2020) *The Complexity of Bird Behaviour: A Facet Theory Approach*, Cham, CH: Springer.

Hackett, P.M.W., Shaw, R.C., Boogert, N.J., and Clayton, N.S. (2019) A Facet Theory Analysis of the Structure of Cognitive Performance in New Zealand Robins (Petroica Longipes), *International Journal of Comparative Psychology*, 32: p1–13.

Shye, S., and Elizur, D. (1994) *Introduction to Facet Theory: Content Design and Intrinsic Data Analysis in Behavioral Research* (Applied Social Research Methods), Thousand Oaks, CA: Sage.

Walton, D. (2001) Abductive, Presumptive and Plausible Arguments, *Informal Logic*, 21(2), 142–169. Retrieved from http://amr.uwindsor.ca/ojs/leddy/index.php/informal_logic/article/view/2241.

Editor's Introduction

Five years ago, I asked David J. Murray to think about writing a history of 19th-century scientific psychology. Over the course of my career, I read many histories of psychology that minimise or sometimes even lack a treatment of psychology as a science, especially with respect to the contributions of mathematics in the early days. Therefore, I looked for an experimental psychologist and historian to help create a more accurate view. I knew of David's translation to English from German of Ernst Heinrich Weber's *Der Tastsinn* (1846) and many other historical articles. I co-authored with David and Helen Ross in 2009 a review of a delightful book on Gustav Fechner by Michael Heidelberger. I felt confident with David's knowledge of history.

A few years later, David provided me a very lengthy manuscript entitled *From Mind to Matter: A History of 19th Century Psychology*. Impressed, I began my first reading. Because of the importance of mathematics in any science, I asked about the manuscript's presentations of mathematical ideas due to Herbart, Fechner, Helmholtz, and others. David informed me that mathematics was not really part of his history.

After my reading of the manuscript, I suggested improvements to show how some missing mathematical ideas were important systems of deep thought about mental processes. David suddenly looked like a sailor standing at the edge of a very rough sea of mathematical equations. He looked sceptically into the distance at one equation then followed by another, very large equation. But his remarkable courage soon revealed itself when he said, "Where's our sailboat?"

We began sailing toward the mathematical representations of mental processes created by Johann Friedrich Herbart (1824). David began the arduous climbing of mathematical ropes, learning to better understand the equations as we sailed along, first a bit against the wind but later on, more smoothly, with the wind at our backs. At the end of our voyage emerged a historian with a remarkable, new, deeper understanding of mathematical reasoning, enriched by his mastery of the German language, especially in its far-from-trivial forms of the 19th century. I thank David for his stellar presentation of the interactions between so many significant historical figures. The result is a new account of the creation of scientific psychology that, we feel, fills a gap in the history of psychology – a new view that we hope will fascinate and excite both lay and experienced readers alike.

Notes

1. I have also applied the facet theory approach to the non-human animals of New Zealand robins (Hackett, 2017b; Hackett et al., 2019) and to birds more generally (Hackett, 2020).
2. This research was conducted in particular reference to how abstract fine art has been experientially conceived in the writing of Crowther (2007). I provide further details of how I have addressed Crowther's understanding of fine art in my research in chapter 3 of this book.

1 Introduction to Mapping Sentences

Content Summary

The mapping sentence is at the heart of the facet theory approach to social research, as it provides a flexible and adaptable descriptive framework through which to understand a research domain (Borg, 1977; Borg and Shye, 1995; Hackett, 2014a). In this first chapter, I provide information about mapping sentences as they have traditionally been used in quantitative facet-theory-based research. In order that the mapping sentence may be better understood, I also provide brief details of the facet theory approach to research. I suggest the need for, and usefulness of, the notion of the mapping sentence within a quantitative research context. Through the use of a mapping sentence as a flexible template to design and analyse research, the results that such research produces address both specific and contextualised research questions whilst yielding comparable results. I therefore start this book by considering the meta-theory from which the traditional mapping sentence is derived: facet theory.

Introduction

The wind really could blow bitingly across Cardigan Bay, the dampness of the Irish Sea adding to the bitter chill and forming a breeze that was able to somehow slice its way through layers of clothes and induce shivers in even the most warm-blooded person. This was what DCI Tom Mathias was thinking about as he walked along the edge of the sand dunes at Ynyslas. He had driven into the nature reserve and parked his car on the beach, which was also the car park for visitors to the reserve and the dunes area in general. There were few cars parked there on a day like today, but there were some hardy souls who were wrapped up and braving the conditions. In the summer, there would be throngs of holiday makers on the beach, but today, the golden sands were practically deserted.

The body was lying on the sand at a point near where the rivers Dyfi and Leri met and formed a flat spit of sand that reached out towards the opposite banks of the estuary and the town of Aberdyfi. "Bora da, Mari, felly beth sydd gyda ni?" Tom shouted to his DI, as he attempted to be heard over the sound of the wind.

"We had better keep it in English, as Bob here doesn't speak Welsh". Bob was a pathologist who was new to the area.

"Sorry, Bob. So what have we got here then, Mari?"

"It looks like a birdwatcher; he has binoculars and a telescope, and he's dressed as if he was a soldier going to war – you know how they dress out here in combat kit so the birds won't see them. His optics are those really expensive Swarovski brand. You know they cost thousands. He seems to have been alone out here, as there are only his footprints near his body, but the thing is he's been strangled with the strap of his binoculars by the look of it".

"I'll have to confirm that later", said Bob, "but that's what it looks like".

"And the body has been here how long?" Tom asked.

"I'd say something less than an hour given the body temperature and the bitter conditions", Bob replied with a furrowed brow and a worried look. He was new to the job, and he hadn't as yet developed a thick skin to death.

"And do we have any witnesses?"

Mari looked at Tom and raised an eyebrow as if to say, "We should be so lucky."

"Not one, and I found the body", she said, "as I was out here taking my usual morning walk".

"I had forgotten you live in Borth, Mari".

"Yes, that's why we were able to get here so quickly. I called Bob directly".

"Any idea who he is?" Tom asked.

"That is a little unusual, Tom. He doesn't appear to be carrying any identification and has no car keys on him. He could have caught the train though".

"And the tide doesn't come this far up the shore, so any footprints would still be here".

"Unless the wind managed to get rid of them", reflected Mari.

Tom stood back from the other two and looked at the body. *So*, he thought, *we have a birdwatcher with no identification and no car keys, alone and dead on the sand. His binoculars and telescope are top end and are still with him. There are no footprints, but these may have been blown away. He's only been dead for an hour, and we have no witnesses.* "Let's get a cordon put up and take in about ten metres around the body. Get the numbers of the cars in the car park and run a check on who they belong to. It's a long shot, but do a house-to-house along the route from the station in Borth. See if anybody saw him on his way out here".

I imagine that quite a few academics, when they are involved in a research project, think of themselves as detectives who are attempting to solve a particularly difficult and intricate case, in the manner of Tom Mathies, the fictional character from the S4C television series *Y Gwyll*, in the preceding example that I dreamt up. Perhaps the detective metaphor works best with the studious detective, such as Tom, rather than the fast-car-driving, gun-toting Los Angeles cop, although there are perhaps some academics who harbour such a fantasy. However, the detective metaphor works best with the clichéd private sleuths: Sherlock Holmes and Watson, Hercules Poirot, and Miss Marple, who jump to mind as investigators who were methodical and thorough in their thinking and investigative activities. Clear thinking and thorough planning are at the roots and heart of research that employs a declarative mapping sentence. In this book, I will be emphasising and illustrating how by using a well-structured approach to asking questions and conducting research, in a manner that is similar to the way of a good detective, researchers are able to conduct investigations that clearly address their research questions and hypotheses and which yield reliable and trustworthy findings.

What Is Facet Theory

I start this book by clearly stating that this book is about how research is conducted in the social sciences and the humanities, with a focus upon one specific approach to this type of research, namely facet theory. More precisely, my writing is largely concerned with the main component of all facet theory research, the mapping sentence, with my interest concentrated upon one form of mapping sentence, the declarative mapping sentence. Much has been written about facet theory, but this is the first book-length consideration of the mapping sentence dissociated from facet theory. In this first chapter, I will begin by providing some information about facet theory and the mapping sentence.

Within the social sciences, facet theory is an approach to research that encompasses research design, data analysis, and theory construction (Guttman, 1959; Borg and Shye, 1995; Tziner, 1987; Hackett, 2014a). Within facet theory, a facet may be understood as being a discretely identifiable aspect of a research area that is under investigation and that may be used to describe or classify this domain. The notion that a domain of interest may be usefully disassembled into pertinent sub-areas in order to facilitate an exploration of the domain is cardinal to the approach. The way in which a domain is described and understood in terms of its components is through the development of a mapping sentence, which constitutes a mereology[1] for a specified research area. The mapping sentence is a framework that allows the proposition of, and investigation into, both the research area's theoretical and its meaningful structure. Furthermore, the mapping sentence facilitates the planning of research designs and the selection of the important sub-areas or variables that will frame later investigations.

The mapping sentence also facilitates the development of the hypotheses or research questions that the research will investigate. In Figure 1.1 is an example of a mapping sentence from Hackett et al. (2011). I will not perform a detailed exploration of this mapping sentence at this point, and I will provide just basic details about this immediately in the following. It is my intention in including this illustration to enable readers who are new to mapping sentences to have an example to refer to as they continue reading.

In Figure 1.1, the mapping sentence describes the definition for a tool to assess the effectiveness of an educational programme that attempts to raise environmental awareness. In this mapping sentence, there are six content facets (facets that define the components that need to be incorporated in an assessment tool), along with a range facet that specifies that any assessment that is made using tools derived from the mapping sentence design will be in terms of the level of confidence those who are implementing the educational programme have that the educational objectives will be met. Finally, the individual completing the assessment tool is specified by the (x) in the opening of the mapping sentence.

Having introduced readers to the mapping sentence, I will now consider the theoretical basis of the mapping sentence.

The Philosophy of Facet Theory

When a research situation involves multiple variables, the facet theory approach may be an appropriate approach to guide the investigation of such a complex existence. Moreover, when using a facet theory approach, the researcher discovers that facet theory plays a significant role at all points of the research process, from designing the project through to analysing and interpreting the data that has arisen from the study's data-gathering procedures and the development or refinement of theories associated with the findings.[2] In fact, the single most pervasive and perhaps most important aspect of research that falls under the facet theory umbrella is the philosophical conceptions that underlie the research: Central to all forms of facet theory enquiries is what may be thought of as a facet theory philosophy. This philosophical stance embodies the belief that research should be explicit, systematic, and undertaken within clearly stated hypotheses that are interrogated directly by the research that is conducted by the scholar. Because of the multifarious nature of facet theory conceptions of behavioural and experiential domains, facet theory hypotheses incorporate not only the multiple variables that are of interest but also statements of the hypothesised structured inter-relationships between the specified variables. These are therefore structural hypotheses and are stated in the form of a mapping sentence.

Facet theory has a widely embracing nature, and if a researcher chooses to use this approach in his or her research, he or she must assume an outlook towards the research subject that embraces a recognition of the complexity

Person (x) assesses the geoscience outreach program which addresses the geoscience issue of

Facet A: Issue		**Facet B: Educational materials**
a_1 - contemporary climate questions a_2 - historical climate change a_3 - learning from past changes a_4 - ameliorating climate change	using the geoscience materials / knowledge regarding	b_1 - climate system b_2 - historical temperature and greenhouse gases trends b_3 - paleorecords

	Facet C: Scientists' objectives	
with the geoscientists' objectives being to achieve	c_1 - initial awareness c_2 -increased awareness c_3 -behavior change	through communications by

Facet D: Communicator		**Facet E: Behavioral objective**
d_1 -scientist d_2 -educator d_3 - psychologist	with the environmental objective of	e_1 - reducing resource consumption e_2 - reducing emissions e_3 - behavioral pledge

	Facet F: Agent	
in a program that is initiated and sustained by	f_1 - the person) f_2 -the institutions	by stating their confidence that the program will mak[e] a positive contribution in terms of the above aims

→ as being { very confident . . . not at all confident }

Figure 1.1 Mapping Sentence for the Design, Implementation, and Monitoring of a Program by Geoscientists to Raise Environmental Awareness (Hackett et al., 2011, p. 222)

of the research situation and the necessity to design research questions and employ analyses that implicate the concurrent effects of multiple variables. Within a facet theory approach, research instruments which investigate the multiple combined effects of variables within a specific area of life are designed. Subsequent to carrying out the research, analyses are conducted that allow the identification of the roles of multiple variables (that are called facets) within the specified life area. The facets are sub-divided into elements that constitute the meaningful variations that are possible within a facet.

For some philosophers, such as William of Ockham and Thomas Hobbes, the only universal aspects of the world are names, where such philosophers understand names to be "a sort of Ariadne's thread to guide us through the labyrinth of sense-impressions" (Mintz, 1962, p. 24). On this understanding, names are the outcomes of reasoning. Moreover, analytical knowledge may arise from arranging and manipulating names in the form of propositions and definitions rooted in our sense-based experiences, which provides greater understanding than sensory information alone. Thus, words are seen as cardinal to our development of knowledge. The mapping sentence is a collection of words that are used to allow greater insight into a research phenomenon. The usefulness of a sentence-based depiction arises from the fact that behaviours, experiences, the state of affairs, or activities may often be conceived as being composed of multiple interacting components that may be described using words in the form of a sentence. When a sentence is an appropriate tool for describing the life area of interest, the researcher who is interested in understanding such phenomena needs to adopt an outlook towards research that recognises the effects of both the multiple individual variables as well as the interactions between variables and their combined effects, as these exist as a phenomenological entirety.

Later in this book, I will spend considerable time talking about mapping sentences of different kinds. However, at this point, I will provide a very brief descriptive introduction to mapping sentences and their constituent components. I will also touch upon facet theory and the analysis of quantitative data that arises from a study that utilises a traditional mapping sentence in its design.

Mapping Sentences

Mapping sentences, as the name suggests, are sentences written as ordinary prose which form a map of research content. Within a mapping sentence, there are a series of facets, which are variables or aspects of the research content that have been identified as being of interest or importance to a research project. The facets are incorporated into the mapping sentence and are joined together using connective words and phrases in a way that suggests the nature of how these facets are related to each other in the meaningful situation of their usual occurrence: in a manner that is phenomenologically valid. At the start of a facet designed research project, a mapping sentence is formulated as a hypothesis of the structural content of the research. The structure is stated in terms of the facets and their elements that are believed to be of importance to the research domain. Facets are written within a mapping sentence in an order and linked together in a way such that the structure of facets in a mapping sentence is also a hypothesis for the domain's semantic structure. The respondents who will be the subject of the research are specified at the start of the sentence, and if quantitative data are to be gathered in the research, this is specified in the range facet at the end of the sentence. The range facet states the type of measures or observations that will be made during the research that will be conducted to investigate the veracity of the specific mapping sentence. In this manner, the mapping sentence spells out the complete research project.

Designing Research Instruments Using Mapping Sentences

When employing a facet theory rubric in conducting a research project, investigatory instruments are designed that incorporate elements of all of the facets in a way that reflects the way the facets have been related to each other in the mapping sentence. To do this, one element is selected from each and every facet and used to design an individual question, observation, or other form of data gathering. In doing this, the content of the instruments is reflective of combinations of the facet elements, which are brought together in a manner that corresponds to the hypothesised relationships between the facets in the study's mapping sentence.

The mapping sentence in Figure 1.2 is a general mapping sentence for a person's experience of health. This mapping sentence is extremely terse and possesses no connective words or phrases between the facets and their elements. This "general" mapping sentence simply states the variables that are considered to be important to the experience of health. Indeed, in linguistic terms, this is not a sentence and does not convey any real world sense of how a person may actually experience the phenomena of being well or ill. However, it should be noted that the general mapping sentence does not explicitly attempt to phenomenologically locate the subject matter of the sentence but rather to specify and delimit the variables of interest to the study.

In Figure 1.2, the person reports his or her experience as being somewhere between extremely ill to well (shown in the range facet at the end of the

The extent to which a person describes him/herself as being:

[physically]	[ill]	[in the future]		
[emotionally]	[well]	[at present]		extremely ill
[socially]		[in the recent past]	→	
		[in the longer past]		well

Figure 1.2 A General Mapping Sentence for Health (Canter and Nanke, 1993)

sentence). This evaluation is in reference to the three content facets that any specific health or illness experience may be related to his or her physical, emotional, or social health or illness in the future, present, recent past, or long past.

Canter and Nanke (1993) stated that their mapping sentence contained three levels of interrelated hypotheses. In this mapping sentence, the chronicity of their health problems, be this over the shorter or longer term, will be experienced differently and will yield distinct responses to enquiries regarding chronically distinct health issues. Also in this example, a category of distinction between health issues will also exist in terms of the type of symptom being social, physical, or emotional. They said that the most fundamental hypothesis contained in their mapping sentence was that positive aspects of health are not the same phenomena as negative aspects of health but are instead interacting but different processes: "One is the process of debilitation and illness. The other is the process of enrichment and life enhancement" (Canter and Nanke, 1993, p. 144).

In their mapping sentence, as well as the hypothesis regarding the elements of the facets constituting separately distinguishable aspects of the phenomenon under scrutiny (in this case health), there is a hypothesis that addresses the relationships between facets' elements. The authors provide examples of how in their mapping sentence the elements of the symptoms facet may be experienced in specific ways. For example, emotional symptoms may be seen as being centrally related to both physical experiences and social experiences, and thus there may exist an ordering of elements from physical to social. The temporal facet may also be ordered in a similar way from current experiences to experiences from the recent past to experiences from the more distant past.

In reading the last paragraph, you may be disagreeing with my suggested configuration for facet elements. Such a disagreement is the proper belief to take, as what I am stating is conjecture and research must be conducted to support or refute the structure of my proposed hypotheses. The elements that the authors suggest may be redundant, and other elements may be found to be more pertinent. The proposed arrangement of elements may also need modification. Furthermore, the authors note how different types of illness and well-being will be experienced differentially, although the facets together constitute the systematic experience of health, and it is possible to propose that some aspects of health-related experience will be central to such experiences and embody its essence.

It may be useful to provide an analogy as an example of the systemic nature of health experience by considering a laptop upon which I am working, which has many components, each of which performs a different function – for example, the screen, the keyboard, and the electronic components inside the laptop. The first of these allows input from me, the screen allows the sharing of my input back with me to allow editing, and the latter component brings these two functions together and makes the laptop work as a laptop. However, when these units of the laptop are brought together in a specific manner, they suggest specific characteristics of the laptop, such as its quality or its processing abilities. Here, the memory size or processing speed are central and vital to how the laptop performs as a system and how the specific features of the laptop may be experienced. However, whilst this may be a useful analogy for the systematic experience of health, the structure and centrality of health and well-being may vary at different times and may be related to specific illnesses and treatments that a person is undergoing.

The preceding "general" mapping sentence provides a specification of the hypotheses noted earlier; however, it is the bare minimum of health experience and does not embody health and illnesses experiences in any real-world sense. We do not experience health and illness as a series of unattached, non-contextualised variables, as is implied in the general mapping sentence given in Figure 1.2. In order to represent health and illness in a more lived context, the general mapping sentence must be turned into a traditional mapping sentence or declarative mapping sentence that may be used to understand specific experiences that people have through the incorporation of connective words and phrases between the facets.

For example, a mapping sentence from which research could be designed and interpreted in the area of how people experience health may read as follows:

By providing connective phrases between the facets, I have placed the mapping sentence into a more realistic context, one that may reflect the reality of health experiences. These structural arrangements are a further form of hypothesis that is contained in a mapping sentence, and, importantly, they are essential to the understanding and use of the mapping sentence in qualitative research in the form of the declarative mapping sentence, which I will concentrate on later in this book.

If there is any doubt about the veracity of my claims that connective words and phrases are both needed and absolutely essential in using mapping sentences, then consider the following example:

The two mapping sentences in Figures 1.3 and 1.4 contain the same facets and elements, but the connective phrases and the ordering of facets are different. With these changes, which some may see as peripheral alterations, any research instrument that is developed from one of the mapping sentences will be different to those designed using the other mapping sentence. Furthermore, the understanding and knowledge that grows out of these two mapping sentences will not be the same.

I am going to close my initial consideration of mapping sentences by presenting another example, this time from the early days of facet theory research. I present this illustration by Rimoldi (1951), as it is still quite simple but more sophisticated than the previous two examples. In his mapping sentence, he presents an account of a framework for selecting and defining

		Symptom
Person (x) describes that he or she is feeling:		(physically)
		(emotionally)
		(socially)

Modality	
(ill)	and that they have or will experience this is the:
(well)	

Chronicity		**Range**
(long past)	by stating that they are:	(well)
(recent past)		(to)
(present)		(extremely ill)
(future)		

Figure 1.3 Traditional Mapping Sentence for Health

the items that are included in an intelligence test in terms of how these are parts of sub-tests of intelligence (see Figure 1.5).

Intelligence and the development of items for intelligence tests have used a variety of definitions and tools. I am not going to consider these and other issues associated with the nature of intelligence and how to assess this; I am simply providing two definitions that represent an account for the content of intelligence which can be used to develop intelligence test items. In a manner that is similar to Canter and Nanke's (1993) in relationship to the experience of health, Louis Guttman and Schlomitt Levy (1991) produced a general mapping sentence for intelligence (see Figure 1.6).

Rimoldi's mapping sentence has the same response range as does the mapping sentence by Guttman and Levy: Both mapping sentences specify that when taking an intelligence test, the person being tested may get the test right or wrong as this is established by some pre-stated rule. However, rather than simply defining what theoretically constitutes an intelligence test item, Rimoldi provides details of the types of items that may be found in an intelligence test battery. In Guttman's mapping sentence, there is a

Modality

Person (x) describes that he or she is feeling/have felt either: (ill)
(well)

Chronicity

and that experience is the: (long past)
(recent past)
(present)
future

Symptom

and that these feelings are being/ have been expressed: (physically)
(emotionally)
(socially)

Range

by and have resulted in them being: (well)
(to)
(extremely ill)

Figure 1.4 Traditional Mapping Sentence for Health

single facet that stipulates that any intelligence test item may ask a person to employ either a logical, factual, or semantic rule. Rimoldi expands upon this rudimentary structure through the inclusion of three facets, which he labels A, B, and C. Facet A stipulates the way in which the test item is completed (in this case, he simply lists paper and pencil completion). Facet B states that a test item is in a form that employs verbal, numerical, or geometrical language that requires the individual completing the item to use either inference, application, or learning (Facet C) in order to successfully meet the criteria of the objective rule in his or her performance.

Residing behind all facet theory analyses is the motion that individual questions, observations, and other forms of data-gathering procedures that are designed with a mapping sentence are psychologically more alike if

A

The performance of testee (x) through: (3. Paper and pencil) expression on

B

(1. verbal)
an item presented with the aid of: (2. numerical) language, and requiring:
(3. geometrical)

C *R*

(1. inference) (very right)
(2. application) of an objective rule, → (to) performance
(3. learning) (very wrong)

according to the rule.

Legend:
A = testing/assessment format
B = language / medium of presentation
C = required intellectual ability
R = Range

Figure 1.5 Mapping Sentence for Intelligence Subtests (Rimoldi, 1951)

An item belongs to the universe of intelligence items, if and only if its domain asks

(logical)
about: (scientific [factual]) objective rule, and its range is ordered from:
(semantic)

(very right)
(to) with respect to that rule.
(very wrong)

Figure 1.6 General Mapping Sentence for Human Intelligence Items (Guttman and Levy, 1991)

they have had similar facet elements in their design. Conversely, individual questions and so on that have been compiled using different facet elements will be of greater dissimilarity.

Quantitative Facet Theory Analysis

In facet theory, as it has traditionally been used, the data that is collected has been quantitative. This has been numerically specified in the range facet. The range facet appears at the end of a traditional mapping sentence and states the values that will be taken by the instruments that have been designed using the mapping sentence. Permutation of facet element combinations within a mapping sentence will be evaluated by respondents and given a value from the specified range facet. The numerical data gathered is then analysed using the multidimensional statistical techniques of smallest space analysis (SSA), multidimensional scalogram analysis (MSA), and partial order scalogram analysis with base co-ordinates (POSAC or POSA). Smallest space analysis is the most frequently used form of quantitative analysis employed in facet theory designed research. SSA commences by correlating all responses gathered from the research instrument used in a study. Responses to each research question, observation, and so on are then printed within a series of two-dimensional plots. In each plot, the distance between the research items (for example, the questions asked) approximately corresponds to the inverse magnitude of the correlation coefficient between the responses received for the two items. This relationship is present between each and every pairing of research items in a study. Lines (that are straight or regularly curved) are then drawn to partition the items into spatial regions that, as much as is possible, exclusively and comprehensively capture items that are characterised by having a similar facet element. Through the use of SSA, the psychological construction of the research domain is depicted in terms of how respondents report experiencing similarities and differences present within this content.

So far in this book, I have used examples from human behaviour to illustrate a facet theory approach to research. However, in order to demonstrate the theory's flexibility, the illustration I give of quantitative analysis procedures will come from my own research into bird behaviour (Hackett, 1983; Hackett et al., 2017a, 2019, 2020).

In this research, my colleagues and I used facet theory to investigate the cognitive performance of New Zealand robins[3] (*Petroica longipes*) and analysed the arising data using smallest space analysis (SSA) and partial order scalogram analysis (POSA). The data set was from the execution of a test-battery to assess avian cognitive performance that was gathered by Shaw et al. (2015). Twenty adult free-flying New Zealand robins (*Petroica longipes*) (males 14, females 4, sex unknown 2) took part, but three birds went missing before the end of the assessment. The test battery was made up of six tasks that were given to the birds in the following order: (1) motor task; (2) colour discrimination; (3) colour reversal; (4) spatial memory; (5) inhibitory control; and (6) symbol discrimination, all of which were measured in terms of trials before meeting a criterion. Items were first intercorrelated, and these statistics were found to be positive of varying degrees with four very small negative associations. The negative correlations suggested that motor task was accessing a slightly different type of performance to the remaining tasks.

Smallest Space Analysis (Two-Facet Solution)

Hackett et al. (2019) used smallest space analysis (SSA), which produced an extremely accurate two-facet solution (CoA [0.00000]). The first facet discovered was a facet with three distinct regions or elements in an axial configuration. The elements were of different task types: new learning, colour discrimination, and memory and inhibition. The axial arrangement demonstrated an ordered difference between the skills that the birds used, where some skills were different from some of the other skills but more similar to other skills needed to complete other tasks (Figure 1.7).

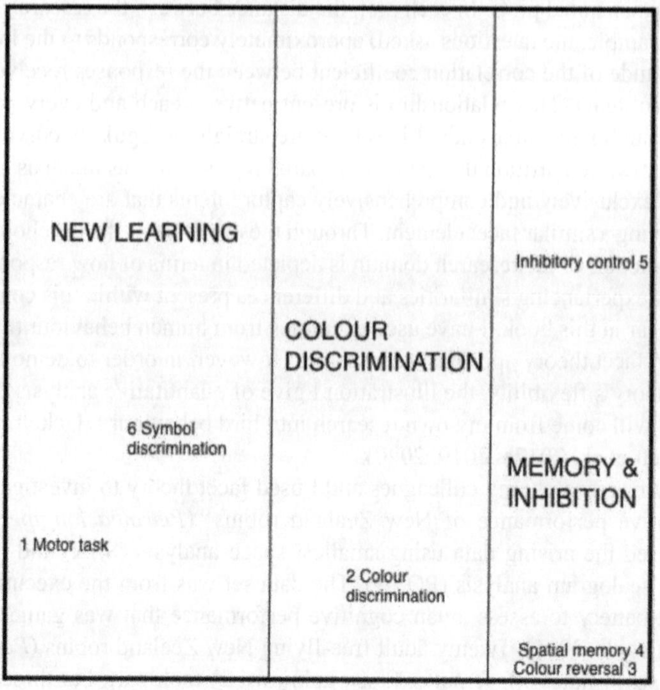

Figure 1.7 Space Diagram for Two-Facet SSA: Task-Type Facet (Hackett et al., 2019)

A second, modular structure facet, was also found (Figure 1.8). This modular facet demonstrated that some skills were more central/general and others more peripheral/particular. This configuration was due to some items being more strongly associated with all other items and therefore more centrally positioned in the plot. The motor task item was centrally positioned, which suggested that the skills involved in performing this task were, at least to a moderate extent, associated with all of the other skills being assessed. The researchers lent support to the veracity of the centrality of the motor task item in the printout from the SSA when they commented that birds were trained to perform the motor task prior to their learning the other tasks and that performance of motor task skills were essential to successful completion of other tasks. Overall, the second facet was found to focus task performance by the centrality/generality versus peripherality/particularity of the skills employed in the successful completion of the six tasks in the test battery.

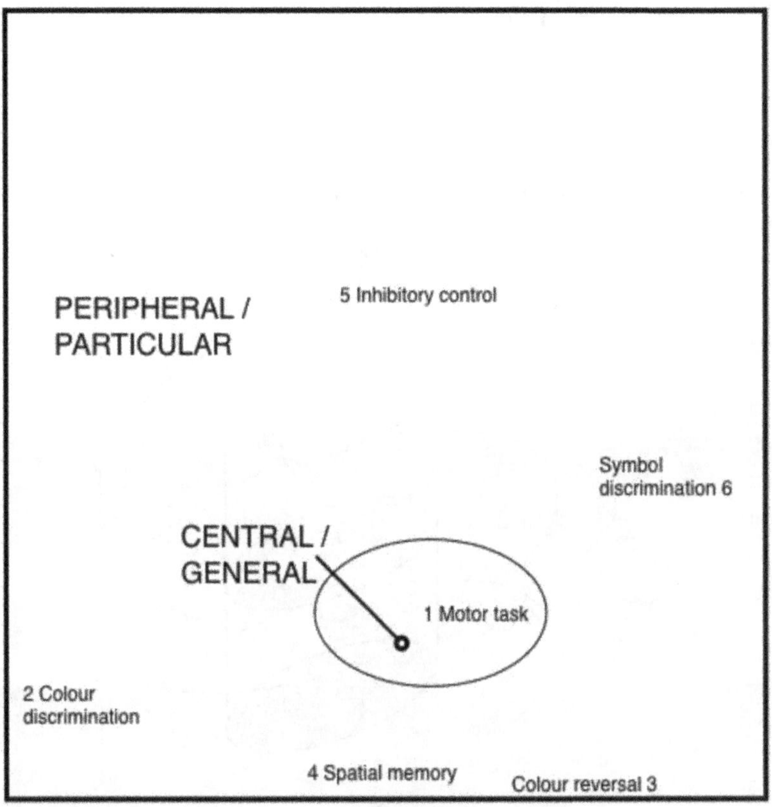

Figure 1.8 Space Diagram for Two-Facet SSA: Focus Facet (Hackett et al., 2019)

From the SSA, the authors developed a mapping sentence for avian cognitive performance (Figure 1.9).

Hackett et al. (2019) developed a model in the form of a cylindrex to display how the effects of the two facets could be thought of as interacting together (Figure 1.10). The cylindrex showed how the facet that contained

	Task Type
	(new learning)
The response from Robin (x) that required the use of:	(colour discrimination)
	(memory and inhibition)

	Focus	
skills, that are:	(peripheral/particular)	to the completion of the task,
	(central/general)	

	Range
	(correct)
were assessed to be:	(to)
	(incorrect)

Figure 1.9 Mapping Sentence for Avian Cognitive Performance

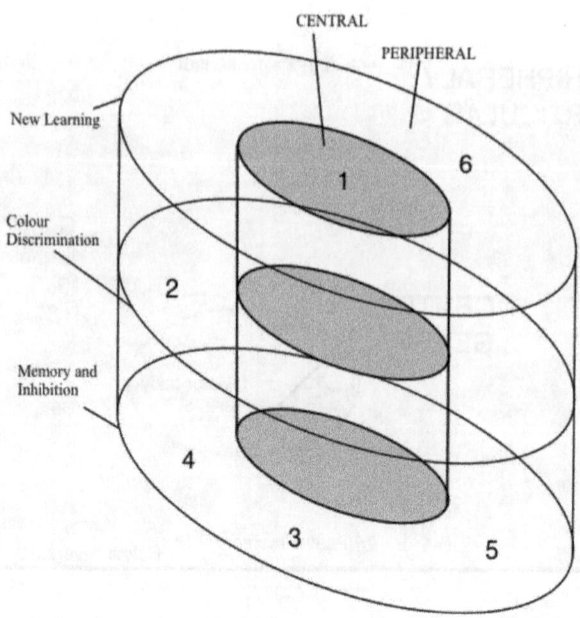

Figure 1.10 Two-Facet Cylindrex (Hackett et al., 2019)

the elements of central and peripheral tasks and focused assessments of performance could be depicted in an orthogonal relationship with the types of skills facet. The relationship was orthogonal, as the facets were found in two separate plots rather than in a single plot and demonstrated that they had independent effects.

Partial Order Scalogram Analyses

The second common form of quantitative facet analysis the authors employed was that of POSA. In this form of analysis, instead of plotting items, respondents were plotted, and in this research, it was the individual birds which were represented as numbers (Figure 1.11).

There are two axes in a Hasse diagram (which is the name for the diagram in Figure 1.11). In this example, a dimension ran from the bottom left to the top right of the diagram which positioned birds in terms of their summated scores on all tasks, with individual birds with low summated scores at the bottom left. In this example, the highest summated scores were achieved by birds numbered 1, 2, 3, and 4 and the lowest by bird 16. The second dimension ran from the bottom right to the top left of the diagram, and on this dimension, birds with similar responses on individual test items were plotted close together within exclusive regions. The lines in the diagram were drawn in order to capture similar scores on each task (which initially were presented on separate plots and them combined in the Hasse diagram and which are indicated by different colours). The lines that are drawn can only be of a limited number of shapes and must be straight. They may be vertical, horizontal, an "L" shape (of the type shown by SM in the Hasse diagram), or an inverted "L" shape (shown by CD in the plot).

The lines' direction and shape demonstrated how the individual tasks in Hackett et al.'s assessment related to a bird's overall performance and also how the tasks were related to each other. In the present example, the motor task (MT) and symbol discrimination task (SD) were partitioned with horizontal lines that demarcate space into vertical regions. When different items divide space up in a similar direction or shape, they indicate that the cognitive performance of these tasks is similar. Inhibition control (I) and colour reversal (CR) tasks partitioned space in the diagram in the opposite direction to the MT and SD tasks: Partitioned regions that run orthogonally to each other demonstrate relative independence. The partitioning of inhibition (I) and colour reversal (CR) (horizontal regions) and motor task (MT) and symbol discrimination (SD) (vertical regions) were opposite to each other, and they played independent roles in task completion. Tasks that can be partitioned into "L" or inverted "L" regions (SM and CD respectively) had a moderating role in association with tasks that were partitioned either vertically or horizontally, where the two orientations of the "L" partitioning had a moderating effect in opposite directions to each other and the tasks played qualitatively distinct roles.

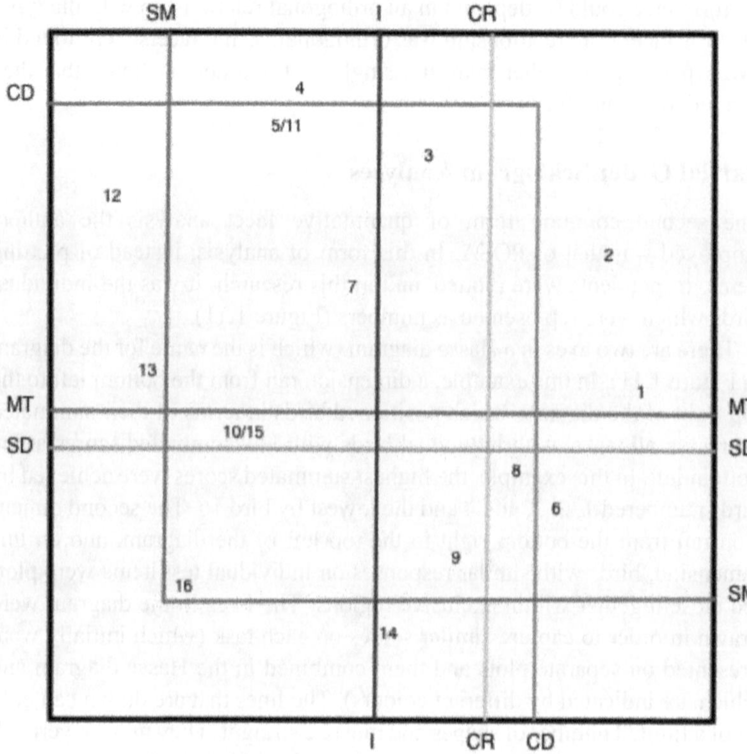

Legend

Task	Abbreviation	Colour	Number in SSA plots
Motor Task	MT		1
Colour Discrimination	CD		2
Colour Reversal	CR		3
Spatial Memory	SM		4
Inhibitory Control	I		5
Symbol Discrimination	SD		6

Figure 1.11 Partitioning for POSA (Hackett et al., 2019)

There are several limitations with the research by Hackett et al. (2019), such as the small number of test items (six), the non-random and small sample of birds, the possibilities of overfitting, and so on. However, the research did show that a two-facet solution accounted for variability in the scores from the test battery, and this was the first use of a facetted approach to the study of wild animals and represents a useful foray into this domain. It also, for the purposes of this book, shows how research data may be quantitatively analysed using both SSA and POSA.

In this section, I have provided a whistle-stop tour of facet theory and the mapping sentence, and I will now consider the mapping sentence in greater detail.

Mapping and Mapping Sentences in Greater Detail

Many different methods exist that enable behaviour and experience to be investigated using multivariate statistical approaches (see, for example, Borg et al., 2013; Hackett and Fisher, 2019; Mertler and Reinhart, 2016; Meyers et al., 2016).[4] However, facet theory is unusual, if not unique, among quantitative multivariate statistical approaches. The peerless aspects of facet theory arise from it constituting a way of statistically analysing multivariate data whilst because of the use of the mapping sentence, with its implicit structural hypotheses, facet theory also involves a theoretical orientation that a researcher can assume towards research design and interpretation which analyses the effects of multiple variables simultaneously and generates hypotheses about the relationships between variables.

If researchers are using a mapping sentence in their design, when they start to think about the multiple variables in their specific research projects, the pertinent variables or facets, along with the elements of each facet, are identified via a variety of means. For example, if the area has been investigated on a previous occasion using a design that employed a facet theory approach, then the research findings reported in this literature will have identified the important and relevant variables, and these will have been stated in a mapping sentence that may be incorporated into the design of the new research. If this is an area or domain that is new to interrogation using facet-theory-designed research, then the researcher will have to conduct a traditional literature search to identify the variables and their sub-conditions that have been found to be relevant within this domain. Finally, the other sources through which variables may be identified are via personal experience and through conducting exploratory research with a sample of respondents who are knowledgeable of the research domain.

Variables and their sub-components are identified in order to attempt to more clearly and precisely understand the particular phenomena that are under investigation. However, once a researcher has disassembled the research domain through the identification of the pertinent variables, he or she will have to re-unite these variables and their associated effects in order that the association between variables and the totality of the research domain may be understood. When conducting research within a facet theory framework, the deconstruction and this re-construction will be in the format of a mapping sentence. Disassembly and reassembly are enabled through the mapping sentence being a clear linguistic statement of the research variables, in which variables are brought together in a way that reflects the meaningful relationship between the variables in terms of the research questions that are being investigated. In the next section of this chapter, I will consider the mapping sentence in greater detail; however, before this, I will spell out the way in which I understand the process of mapping.

Mapping

A map is a diagram or some form of assembly of data which displays how things are spatially arranged across an area. In traditional quantitative use of facet theory, this definition of a map can be imported literally to describe the output from this type of research (using smallest space analysis), which takes the form of a series of statistical diagrams with data spatially distributed across these.[5] Importantly, the word *mapping*, rather than *map*, is used in the phrase *mapping sentence*. Mapping is an active process, and when used in mathematics, it implies associating each and all of the elements present in a set with elements in a second set or range. Thus, in a traditional mapping sentence, the mapping process is a function implying a relation between a set of inputs in the form of facets and their elements and allowable outputs as specified in the range facet. Facet theory's originator Louis Guttman employed the term *mapping* to designate that there is a substantive content which is directly related to the allowable measures of this content. Indeed, Guttman used an arrow to demonstrate the nature of this relationship.

On such an understanding of the contents of a traditional mapping sentence, an input is defined as a facet element combination which is specifically linked with just one value of the range facet output. DuToit et al. (1986, p. 152) wrote this relationship in the following way:

$$X\,ABC \ldots N \rightarrow R$$

When the word *map* is used, it is often indicative of a specific function (such as linearity). Awodey (2010) notes how when the term *mapping* is used in category theory, Simmons (2011) it takes the form of a morphism or an abstraction of a function or a mapping between events in which the mapping structure may be preserved. This is a different type of relationship to that implied by function, which indicates a relationship between a set of inputs and allowable outputs which is shown by the use of an arrow that indicates object relationships. Within the traditional mapping sentence, the range facet is comparable to the concept of the codomain, also taken from mathematics, which is the target of a function. Within a traditional mapping sentence, the range facet determines the permissible responses that arise from enquiries structured by the mapping sentence to fall into the codomain. The mapping sentence specifies how the quantitative analysis of data using a mapping sentence is conducted.[6]

I will now set the scene for a more thorough consideration of the mapping sentence by providing an analogy of the mapping sentence as a series of empty boxes. Dependent upon the domain being investigated and the questions being asked, the researcher establishes the appropriate number of empty boxes, which are the pertinent variables in the research design. The researcher then populates each box with sub-values or conditions of the variable that are pertinent to the domain or area of scholarship. As well as designating boxes that are filled with content relevant to the research, through the use of ordinary prose, the researcher links together the boxes in a way that is meaningful to respondents. An example of an un-populated mapping sentence is provided in Figure 1.12.

In Figure 1.12, the columns are facets (variables) and possess a number of elements (sub-values), which are represented by the column cells. The white columns (which are labelled "prose link") are filled with words and phrases that meaningfully connect the variables and which map the facets into the range facet that is specified at the end of the sentence and is shaded grey. In the illustration, I have included three facets, but there can be any number of

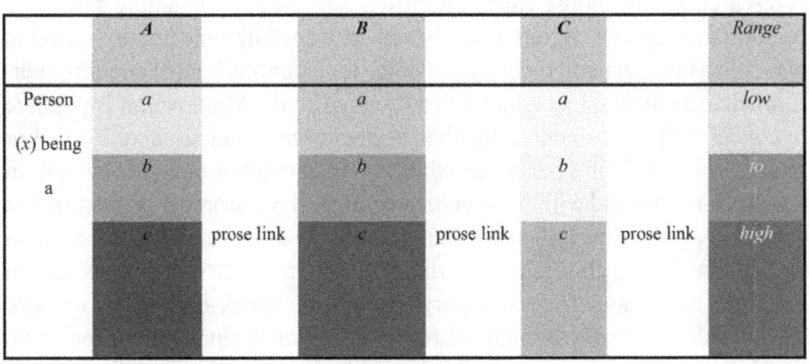

Figure 1.12 Unpopulated Mapping Sentence

facets, the precise number being determined by the research domain of interest and the questions being asked. Each shaded cell in each facet represents an element of the facet, where again the number of elements in a facet is determined by the domain of interest and the way in which this domain is interrogated. The first white column specifies the subjects who will take part in the research, and the second *A* column specifies a background characteristic. There may be no background facets in a specific study, or there may be several. In a traditional mapping sentence, used within a quantitative methodology, the final *range* column will contain the range facet which specifies the measurements that will be taken in the research. In the other columns (in this example *B* and *C*) are the content facets, which are the variables with their sub-values or sub-components chosen to address the research domain and questions of interest.

The traditional mapping sentence has been associated with quantitative research and numerical data and has been used in a wide range of substantive research domains within a variety of theoretical and applied contexts (for examples of the range of subjects addressed, see Ben-Shalom and Horenczyk, 2003; Borg and Shye, 1995; Canter, 1985b; Cardoso, 2018; Fisher, 2014; Greggor and Hackett, 2018; Gurdin, Levy, and Gratch, (1990); Hackett, 2020, 2019a, b, 2018a, b, c, 2017a, b, c, 2016a, b, 2015, 2014a, b, 2013, 1995, 1983; Hackett et al., 2019, 2018, 2016, 2011; Koval et al. 2016; Lou and Hackett, 2018a, b; Ludlow et al., 2014; Maslovaty et al., 2001; Schkoler et al., 2020; Schwarzenbach and Hackett, 2015; Shye, 1978; Shye et al., 1994; Wihlborg et al., 2019; Wu et al., 2015). Before progressing further in considering the application of the mapping sentence, it is useful to initially pay some attention to the theoretical basis of the sentence.

Mapping Sentence Ontology and Mereology

A researcher may choose either a narrowly specified (for example a person's performance upon a cognitive test battery at a specific time and in a specific place) or a more general type of behaviour (for example, human cognitive performance) as their subject matter in a research study. Moreover, it is possible to conceive of the behaviour that has been chosen as being either learned or innate proclivity[7] for a person to exhibit such an overt or covert behaviour in a specific format and within a specified context. If a researcher is interested in cognitive performance, then an example of a behaviour that could be investigated may be the ability for an individual person to perform a block-design task from a psychometric test-battery. The specific block-design performance can be understood to be brought into existence when the inclination along with the ability for a person to assemble plastic blocks to match a two-dimensional image is constituted within specific surroundings and circumstances. Events such as a block-design performance during a cognitive testing situation may be considered as mereologically sophisticated. A block-design performance is a complex occurrence. Therefore, if a researcher wishes to understand a specific block-design performance in terms of it constituting an example of block-design performances in a general sense, the features of the performance, both internal and external to the person performing the task, must be understood in terms of their structural configuration. When considering such a structure of psychological and contextual features, the researcher may ask about the features upon which the mereological structures are contingent. For instance, in what ways do conditions present in a psychometric testing situation, such as the physical testing situation, the relationship of the person being tested with the tester, individual characteristics of the person performing the task, the ambient conditions in the room, and so on combine to form an example of a block-design performance? Furthermore, when considering behaviour under such an understanding, it is the case that performance of a complex behaviour is systemic. If such an understanding is adopted, then in order to provide an adequate answer to questions such as "At what level does a specific person perform a block-design task"? or "How does a specific person's block-design performance relate to block-design performances by other people"?, the researcher asking such questions must consider issues associated with the constitution (ontology) along with the structure (mereology) of the performance. These considerations may be seen to impel a researcher to ask what the fundamental parts of the situation that is being investigated are and how and why these rudimentary structures combine in the way they do in a specified instance with greater or lesser regularity.

In this book, I am interested in the ways in which a mapping sentence may be used in order to provide clarity in terms of the ontological dependence of facets that contingently exist when any specified form of complex behaviour is investigated. Mapping sentences of all forms postulate and denote the parts of a behavioural system along with the essential structural predispositions that influence how parts of the system coexist and vary internally and in relationship to features external to the system.

In a mapping sentence, the words and phrases that a researcher selects to include constitute the most rudimentary parts of the specified research area. As a consequence of their fundamental nature, the chosen content words and phrases in a mapping sentence form an ontology. In this book, I use the term *mereology* to describe a mapping sentence, as a mapping sentence specifies the interrelationships between the components of the mapping sentence as well as the relationships between the components specified and the mapping sentence as a totality of a domain. Furthermore, a mapping sentence may be understood as being a meta-ontology and a meta-mereology, as it is an ontology about ontologies and a mereology about mereologies.

On such an understanding of complex behaviour and existence, it is necessary to specify the rudimentary aspects of a behaviour, state of affairs, experience, and so on, where notions of the relationships between the components of a mapping sentence are essential to the understanding of any specific behaviour, state of affairs, and so on. I therefore claim that mapping sentences provide an understanding of ontologically dependent aspects of a research domain that may be supported by theory and empirical observations. The relationships of the facets and elements within a mapping sentence may be understood in terms of their ontological dependence and truthmaking in terms of the ontology. A truthmaker may be conceived as a substance, quantity, quality, real thing, and so on that has the ability to make a bearer of truth true (Armstrong, 2004). I therefore suggest that within a traditional (quantitative research) mapping sentence, it is the structure of the mapping sentence in conjunction with the range facet which occupies the role of truthmaker in relation to the specific area addressed by the mapping sentence: Mapping sentences are propositional in terms of the features that are important in understanding a research domain. When we later consider the declarative mapping sentence, we will see that this sentence does not necessarily constitute a truth proposition in regard to the content of the sentence, the veracity of which is tested through the realisation of range-specified empirical observations. Rather, the truthmaker of the declarative mapping sentence is the repeated correspondence of the sentence's structure with experience of the state of affairs, behaviour, and so on that is specified in the sentence. Thus, the repeated use of mapping sentences and their ability to provide useful and comparable information that is meaningful within research contexts forms a truthmaker for all types of mapping sentence: It is the discovery of a repeated similar structure for a mapping sentence when applied to a specific research domain that is the mapping sentence's truthmaker. In this way, mapping sentences are propensity ontologies that, because of their explicit specification of ontological components (facets and elements), provide for the comprehensive investigation of the ontology and its constituent parts.

A mapping sentence constitutes what may be seen as an inference that is based upon a series of premises which result in a precise understanding of a specific phenomenon. More precisely stated, facets and facet elements (including background facets) form foundational building blocks that lead to an understanding of the phenomenon under investigation (which in the traditional mapping sentence is expressed through the range facet in quantitative analyses). It is therefore possible to see a mapping sentence as being an argument for the true structure of the phenomenon that a given piece of research is designed to investigate. Moreover, the use of empirical observation and reasoning allows for the mapping sentence to be argued either for or against and to be supported or refuted. Therefore, a mapping sentence constitutes a proposition and an argument whilst it is also an explanation of the phenomenon of interest in reference to how the mapping sentence's content phenomenologically exists.

To summarise what I have said,

1. The facet of subject denotes the individual(s) who will be completing the research.
2. The background facet(s) lists background characteristics that enable the instantiation of the mapping sentence ontology.
3. The content and connective facets (through the selection of the subdivisions of content facet elements and the appropriate selection of connective ontology) specify the substantive content of the mapping sentence.
4. The characteristics of all facets and the nature of the connective relationships that are extant within the mapping sentence ontology are either a part-to-part (facet / facet element to facet / facet element) or part-to-whole (facet / facet element to mapping sentence) mereology.
5. The range facet specifies the epistemological characteristics of the observations and, in part, constitutes the mapping sentence's logic.

Conclusions

As well as being an instrument for designing research inquiries, by providing a precise definition of an area of interest, the mapping sentence establishes the boundaries of the content of interest and is therefore able to determine when a phenomenon does or does not belong to the class of events that are under investigation. The ability to provide precise and meaningful definitions of a research area may help researchers to decide if a phenomenon or event is actually part of the research domain they are investigating or whether it should be removed from the present research. At its best, the mapping sentence unpacks the meaning of the phenomenon and articulates the concept of interest.

The conceptual framework within which researchers or scholars think about the research they undertake is highly influential in the type of scholarship in which they engage, the form of questions they ask, and the ways in which they analyse the information they produce in their research. In this first chapter, I have attempted to provide a description of the mapping sentences with reference to the underlying facet theory approach. I have also made efforts to explain the characteristics of a facetted approach to research activity, and I have attempted to facilitate understanding of the traditional mapping sentence. The components of the mapping sentence have been presented, and I have provided insight into the structure of the mapping sentence through the provision of both textual explanations and diagrams. In attempting to provide an understanding of the traditional mapping sentence, as used in quantitative research, I have only in passing mentioned qualitative research and the declarative mapping sentence (briefly and mainly in footnotes). In Chapter 3, I will consider using declarative mapping sentences in qualitative and philosophical explorations; however, in the next chapter, I will present a short review of how to construct a mapping sentence.

Notes

1. Here mereology is being used as a noun with the meaning the specification of the part-whole relationships for a domain of interest.
2. Whether a research project is designed to collect quantitative, qualitative, or mixed-method information.
3. In Hackett (2020), I expand upon the research presented in this chapter and consider many other ways in which mapping sentences may be used to explore a variety of aspects of birds and their lives.
4. Many authors (for example, Canter, 1985; Levy, 1994) have written upon the development of facet theory, and I will not repeat a rendition of this history in these pages. Instead, I guide the interested reader to the preceding publications and other texts on facet theory.
5. As we will see in chapter 3, when facet theory is used to analyse qualitative information, such descriptive statistics are not the end point of an analysis. However, the notion of a map is still useful when thinking about this form of research, as the aim is to metaphorically map aspects of qualitative information in terms of its relationship with other aspects present in this information in a manner that suggests its spatial arrangement.
6. This is analogous to the thinking present when using a qualitative mapping sentence approach which employs a declarative mapping sentence.
7. A proclivity is here being taken to be an inclination, tendency, or disposition towards behaving in a specified manner. In using the word *proclivity*, I am not favouring a hardwired form of behaviour over a learned behaviour or vice versa.

Further Reading

Those readers who are interested in discovering more about the history of facet theory or traditional quantitative facet theory and mapping sentence research are guided to the following texts:

Borg, I., and Shye, S. (1995) *Facet Theory: Form and Content* (Advanced Quantitative Techniques in the Social Sciences), Thousand Oaks, CA: Sage Publications, Inc.

Canter, D. (ed.) (1985) *Facet Theory: Approaches to Social Research*, New York: Springer Verlag.

Hackett, P.M.W. (2014) *Facet Theory and the Mapping Sentence: Evolving Philosophy, Use and Application*, Basingstoke: Palgrave.

Hackett, P.M.W., and Fisher, Y. (eds.) (2019) *Advances in Facet Theory Research: Developments in Theory and Application and Competing Approaches*, Lausanne, Switzerland: Frontiers Media SA.

Levy, S. (1994) *Louis Guttman on Theory and Methodology: Selected Writings*, London: Routledge.

Maslovaty, N., Marshall, A.E., and Alkin, M.C. (2001) Teachers' Perceptions Structured through Facet Theory: Smallest Space Analysis versus Factor Analysis, *Educational and Psychological Measurement*, 61(1), 71–84.

Rimoldi, H.J.A. (1951) The Central Intellective Factor, *Psychometrika*, 16, 75–101.

Shye, S. (1978) *Theory Construction and Data Analysis in the Behavioral Sciences*, San Francisco: Jossey-Bass.

Shye, S., Elizur, D., and Hoffman, M. (eds.) (1994) *Introduction to Facet Theory: Content Design and Intrinsic Data Analysis in Behavioral Research* (Applied Social Research Methods), Thousand Oaks, CA: Sage Publications, Inc. http://doi.org/10.4135/9781412984645.n6

Tziner, A.E. (1987) *The Facet Analytic Approach to Research and Data Processing*, New York: Peter Lang.

References

Armstrong, D.M. (2004) *Truth and Truthmakers*, Cambridge: Cambridge University Press.

Awodey, S. (2010) Category Theory, Oxford: Oxford University Press.

Ben-Shalom, U., and Horenczyk, G. (2003) Acculturation Orientations: A Facet Theory Perspective on the Bidimensional Model, *Journal of Cross-Cultural Psychology*, 34(2), 176–188.

Borg, I. (1977) Some Basic Concepts of Facet Theory, in Lingoes, J.C. (ed.) (1995) *Geometric Representations of Relational Data: Readings in Multidimensional Scaling*, Ann Arbor, MI: The University of Michigan.

Borg, I., Groenen, P.J.F., and Mair, P. (2013) *Applied Multidimensional Scaling* (Springer Briefs in Statistics), Heidelberg and London: Springer.

Borg, I., and Shye, S. (1995) *Facet Theory: Form and Content* (Advanced Quantitative Techniques in the Social Sciences), Thousand Oaks, CA: Sage Publications, Inc.

Canter, D. (1985) How to Be a Facet Researcher, in Canter, D. (ed.) *Facet Theory: Approaches to Social Research*, New York: Springer Verlag, 265–276.

Canter, D., and Nanke, L. (1993) Can Health Be a Quantitative Criterion? A Multi-Facet Approach to Health Assessment, in Lafaille, R., and Fulder, S. (eds.) *Towards a New Science of Health*, London: Routledge, 142–155.

Cardoso, M. (2018) Occupational Risks: Perceptual Map Construction Using Psychometric Paradigm and Multivariate Methods, *Independent Journal of Management & Production*, 9(3), 750–766.

duToit, S.H.C., Steyn, A.G.W., & Stumpf, R.H. (1986) Graphical Exploratory Data Analysis, Springer Texts in Statistics, New York: Springer Verlag.

Fisher, Y. (2014) The Timeline of Self-efficacy: Changes During the Professional Life Cycle of School Principals, *Journal of Educational Administration*, 52(1), 58–83.

Greggor, A.L., and Hackett, P.M.W. (2018) Categorization by the Animal Mind, in Hackett, P.M.W. (ed.) *Mereologies, Ontologies and Facets: The Categorial Structure of Reality*, Lanham, MA: Lexington Publishers.

Guttman, L. (1959) Introduction to Facet Design and Analysis, in *Proceedings of the Fifteenth International Congress of Psychology*, Amsterdam: North Holland, 130–132.

Guttman, L., and Levy, S. (1991) Two Structural Laws for Intelligence, Intelligence, 15, 79–109.

Hackett, P.M.W. (1983) *Observations on Blink Rates in Ferruginous Duck (Aythya Nyroca) in a Flock of Mainly Mallard (Anas Platyrhynchos)*, Working Paper/Field Notes.

Hackett, P.M.W. (1995) *Conservation and the Consumer: Understanding Environmental Concern*, London: Routledge Publishers.

Hackett, P.M.W. (2013) *Fine Art and Perceptual Neuroscience: Field of Vision and the Painted Grid, Explorations in Cognitive Psychology Series*, London: Psychology Press.

Hackett, P.M.W. (2014a) *Facet Theory and the Mapping Sentence: Evolving Philosophy, Use and Application*, Basingstoke: Palgrave.

Hackett, P.M.W. (2014b) A Facet Theory Model for Integrating Contextual and Personal Experiences of International Students, *Journal of International Students*, 4(2), 164–176.

Hackett, P.M.W. (2015) Classifying Reality, by David S. Oderberg (ed.) (2013) Chichester: Wiley-Blackwell, *Frontiers in Psychology, Section Theoretical and Philosophical Psychology*, 6, 461. https://doi.org/10.3389/fpsyg.2015.00461.

Hackett, P.M.W. (2016a) *Psychology and Philosophy of Abstract Art: Neuroaesthetics, Perception and Compensation*, Basingstoke: Palgrave.

Hackett, P.M.W. (2016b) Facet Theory and the Mapping Sentence as Hermeneutically Consistent Structured Meta-Ontology and Structured Meta-Mereology, *Frontiers in Psychology, Section Theoretical and Philosophical Psychology*, 7, 471. https://doi.org/10.3389/fpsyg.2016.00471.

Hackett, P.M.W. (2017a) Commentary: Wild Psychometrics: Evidence for 'General' Cognitive Performance in Wild New Zealand Robins, Petroica Longipes, *Frontiers in Psychology, Section Theoretical and Philosophical Psychology*, 8, 165. https://doi.org/10.3389/fpsyg.2017.00165.

Hackett, P.M.W. (2017b) Editorial: Conceptual Categories and the Structure of Reality: Theoretical and Empirical Approaches, *Frontiers in Psychology, Section Theoretical and Philosophical Psychology*, 8, 601. https://doi.org/10.3389/fpsyg.2017.00601.

Hackett, P.M.W. (2017c) Opinion: A Mapping Sentence for Understanding the Genre of Abstract Art Using Philosophical/Qualitative Facet Theory, *Frontiers in Psychology, section Theoretical and Philosophical Psychology*, October 2017, 8, DOI: 10.3389/fpsyg.2017.01731

Hackett, P.M.W. (2018a) Declarative Mapping Sentence Mereologies: Categories from Aristotle to Lowe, in Hackett, P.M.W. (ed.) *Mereologies, Ontologies and Facets: The Categorial Structure of Reality*, Lanham, MD: Lexington Publishers.

Hackett, P.M.W. (2018b) Introduction. Theoretical and Applied Categories in Philosophy and Psychology, in Hackett, P.M.W. (ed.) *Mereologies, Ontologies and Facets: The Categorial Structure of Reality*, Lanham, MD: Lexington Books.

Hackett, P.M.W. (2018c) Declarative Mapping Sentences as a Co-ordinating Framework for Qualitative Health and Wellbeing Research, *Journal of Social Science & Allied Health Professions, 2:1*, E1–E6.

Hackett, P.M.W. (2019a) Facet Mapping Therapy: The Potential of a Facet Theoretical Philosophy and Declarative Mapping Sentences within a Therapeutic Setting, *Frontiers in Psychology, Section Psychology for Clinical Settings*. https://doi.org/10.3389/fpsyg.2019.0122.

Hackett, P.M.W. (2019b) Declarative Mapping Sentences as a Co-ordinating Framework for Qualitative Health and Wellbeing Research, *Journal of Social Science & Allied Health Professions*, 2(1), E1–E6.

Hackett, P.M.W. (2020) *The Complexity of Bird Behaviour: A Facet Theory Approach*, Cham, CH: Springer.

Hackett, P.M.W., Lou, L., and Capobianco, P. (2018) Integrating and Writing-up Data Driven Quantitative Research: From Design to Result Presentation, in Hackett, P.M.W. (ed.) *Quantitative Research Methods in Consumer Psychology: Contemporary and Data Driven Approaches*, London: Routledge.

Hackett, P.M.W., Schwarzenbach, J.B., and Jurgens, A.M. (2016) *Consumer Psychology: A Study Guide to Qualitative Research Methods*, Leverkusen: Barbara Budrich Publishers.

Hackett, P.M.W., Sepúlveda, J., and McCarthy, K. (2011) Improving Climate Change Education: A Geoscientific and Psychological Collaboration, in Fisher, Y., and Friedman, I.A. (eds.) *New Horizons for Facet Theory: Searching for Structure in Content Spaces and Measurement*, Israel: FTA Publications, 219–226.

Hackett, P.M.W., Shaw, R.C., Boogert, N.J., and Clayton, N.S. (2019) A Facet Theory Analysis of the Structure of Cognitive Performance in New Zealand Robins (Petroica Longipes), *International Journal of Comparative Psychology, 32:* p1–13.

Koval, E.M., Hackett, P.M.W., and Schwarzenbach, J.B. (2016) Understanding the Lives of International Students: A Mapping Sentence Mereology, in Bista, K., and Foster, C. (eds.) *International Student Mobility, Services, and Policy in Higher Education*, IGI Global Publishers.

Levy, S. (ed.) (1994) *Louis Guttman on Theory and Methodology: Selected Writings*, Aldershot: Dartmouth Publishing Company.

Lou, L., and Hackett, P.M.W. (2018a) *The Facet Theory Approach to Social Research, Contemporary Data Interpretations: Empirical Contributions in the Organizational Context*. Organization 4.1: The Role of Values in Organizations of the 21st Century.

Lou, L., and Hackett, P.M.W. (2018b) *Qualitative Facet Theory and the Declarative Mapping Sentence, Contemporary Data Interpretations: Empirical Contributions in the Organizational Context*. Organization 4.1: The Role of Values in Organizations of the 21st Century.

Ludlow, L.H., Matz-Costa, C., Johnson, C., Brown, M., Besen, E., and James, J.B. (2014) Measuring Engagement in Later Life Activities: Rasch-Based Scenario Scales for Work, Caregiving, Informal Helping, and Volunteering, Measurement and Evaluation, *Counseling and Development*, 47(2), 127–149.

Mertler, C.A., and Reinhart, R.V. (2016) *Advanced and Multivariate Statistical Methods* (6th ed.), London: Routledge.

Meyers, L.S., Gamst, G., and Guarino, A.J. (2016) *Applied Multivariate Research: Design and Interpretation*, Thousand Oaks, CA: Sage.

Mintz, S.I. (1962) *The Hunting of Leviathan: Seventeenth-Century Reactions to the Materialism and Moral Philosophy of Thomas Hobbes*, Cambridge: Cambridge University Press.

Schwarzenbach, J.B., and Hackett, P.M.W. (2015) *Transatlantic Reflections on the Practice-Based Ph.D. in Fine Art*, New York: Routledge Publishers.

Shaw, R. C., Boogert, N. J., Clayton, N. S., & Burns, K. C. (2015) Wild Psychometrics: evidence for 'general' cognitive performance in wild New Zealand robins, Petroica longipes. *Animal Behaviour 109*, (2015) 101–111.

Shkoler, O., Rabenu, E., Hackett, P.M.W., and Capobianco, P.M. (2020) *International Student Mobility and Access to Higher Education* (Marketing and Communication in Higher Education), Basingstoke: Palgrave MacMillan.

Shye, S. (1978) *Theory Construction and Data Analysis in the Behavioral Sciences*, San Francisco, CA: Jossey-Bass.

Shye, S., Elizur, D., and Hoffman, M. (eds.) (1994) *Introduction to Facet Theory: Content Design and Intrinsic Data Analysis in Behavioral Research* (Applied Social Research Methods), Thousand Oaks, CA: Sage Publications, Inc. http://doi.org/10.4135/9781412984645.n6.

Simmons, H. (2011) *An Introduction to Category Theory*, Cambridge: Cambridge University Press.

Tziner, A.E. (1987) *The Facet Analytic Approach to Research and Data Processing*, New York: Peter Lang.

Wihlborg, J., Edgren, G., Johansson, A., Sivberg, B., and Gummesson, C. (2019) Using the Case Method to Explore Characteristics of the Clinical Reasoning Process Among Ambulance Nurse Students and Professionals, *Nurse Education in Practice*, 35, 48–54.

Wu, J., Kim, A., and Koo, J. (2015) Co-design Visual Merchandising in 3D Virtual Stores: A Facet Theory Approach, *Journal of Retail & Distribution Management*, 43(6), 538–560.

2 Constructing a Mapping Sentence

Content Summary

In this chapter, I offer a user's guide on how to construct a mapping sentence (both traditional and declarative). To illustrate the development *from scratch*, I focus on a specified research domain – in this example, people's experience of place – and I develop a mapping sentence that addresses this area. I provide an illustrative example of how to produce a mapping sentence for a research study that comprises multiple variables and is set in the context of this experientially complex domain. Facet theory and mapping sentences are most commonly used in situations in which intricate research designs are produced to investigating the simultaneous effects of multiple variables. However, I commence by stating a single independent and dependant variable research design. I then make the research design progressively more intricate through the incorporation of other variables. I also develop both a declarative mapping sentence and a traditional mapping sentence for this research area. After readers complete this chapter, it should be obvious how to construct a mapping sentence. I additionally emphasise the value of using the mapping sentence to produce a standardised framework within which to design and analyse complex research questions. Finally, I emphasise that the template offered by a mapping sentence results in the development of consistent and comparable results and the origination of knowledge in the area of study.

Introduction

My aims in this chapter are to offer an example of the way that a researcher may produce a mapping sentence that could guide investigation for the area of research interest when no previous mapping sentence exists. This chapter will form a user's guide to producing a mapping sentence that a neophyte mapping sentence researcher may adapt and use in his or her own research.

It is also my hope that through the process of developing a mapping sentence, a researcher will come to better understand the concepts and theoretical basis behind the use of mapping sentences in research.

At the start of a research project into behaviour, experiences, and so on, a psychologist, social researcher, and so on is likely to commence by undertaking a comprehensive review of the literature pertinent to the area of interest. This form of review is undertaken to reveal the current knowledge about the event, to suggest areas in which knowledge is lacking, and to provide insight into how research may be undertaken aimed at filling such gaps in knowledge. In a slightly more formal sense, the literature review may allow the statement of valid and relevant hypotheses about the event. Once the hypotheses and questions for a study have been developed, research methods and designs are chosen that will best allow the testing of hypotheses and answering of the research questions. The methods and designs that are chosen may be in the form of observations, experiments, case studies, and many other approaches. Having gathered and analysed the resulting data, the researcher accepts or rejects the study's hypotheses or offers answers to the research's initial questions. However, as well as answering the questions that motivated the specific study, attempts are made to generalise the results to a wider population than the study's sample. Arising out of the desire to generalise research findings in this way, results are interpreted and related to wider extant theories that offer explanations that are applicable beyond the bounds of the study's sample. The mapping sentence provides hypotheses about the variables that are expected to be of importance to the research along with their predicted interrelationships. These structural hypotheses are proposed in the form of a mapping sentence, and I will now turn to how this is constructed.

Constructing a Mapping Sentence

In this chapter, I provide a guide to developing a mapping sentence that assumes no previous experience of working with mapping sentences. Later, I will address how to develop a traditional mapping sentence, but first, I illustrate how to progress a declarative mapping sentence.

A Declarative Mapping Sentence

In the first chapter of this book, I gave brief details about mapping sentences and facet theory, and in order to facilitate understanding of mapping sentences and also to enable this chapter to be read alone, I may repeat some of the content of Chapter 1 in this chapter. Developing a declarative mapping sentence is a process that involves the definition of a research domain. The declarative mapping sentence *is* this definition, which is made up of specified research variables or aspects of the research domain that are thought to be important in our understanding of the domain within a research framework. Subsequent to the formulation of this definition, research instruments are produced based upon the structure of this declarative mapping sentence (see also Hackett, 2014; Maslovaty et al., 2001; Maslovaty and Levy, 2001; Shirom, 1991). The use of the declarative mapping sentence[1] is rooted in the belief that it is of cardinal importance that valid and robust concepts are used in order to clearly define a research area and that the format of a declarative mapping sentence is appropriate to achieve these ends (see, Borg and Shye, 1995; Canter, 1985b; Guttman, 1947, 1954a, b, 1959a, b, 1971; Guttman and Greenbaum, 1998; Hackett, 2014, 2020). When designing a declarative mapping sentence for a research project, the area that the research is addressing is termed the *content universe* or the *content domain.*

During the opening stage of the formation of a declarative mapping sentence, the researcher undertakes the meticulous specification of all pertinent variables or discrete aspects of the research area (facets). This initial stage may take some time, as the researcher is attempting to collect all facets that logically and completely describe how people understand and experience the domain of interest. In the present example, I am considering place experience and the investigation of this. The scholar attempting such research then attempts to identify the facets that have been discovered and reported in the literature, for example, about place experience.[2] The scholar then tries to isolate facets that are independent from each other and assembles these in a way that unambiguously illustrates the way in which these facets relate to the other facets and to the overall experience of place.

Having identified from the literature the important facets of place experience, the researcher divides each facet into a complete and exhaustive set of sub-units (elements). Each of these elements should be the mutually exclusive conditions or states that the facet can assume. The importance of identifying the appropriate facets and facet elements and that these are mutually exclusive and comprehensive is shown when one considers how facet theory was formulated under the implicit notion that human activities and knowledge about these are constituted of discrete and identifiable components (e.g., Guttman, 1947). In the following example, I illustrate this in attempting to design research and to understand place experience.

It may seem to be an additional and onerous task for a researcher to have to design any mapping sentence prior to commencing research. However, in the following section, I provide an illustration of how to develop a declarative mapping sentence which will, I hope, start to demonstrate the usefulness of going through this rigorous procedure. In my illustration, I commence by developing an extremely simple piece of research in which only one facet (variable) is included. Such a rudimentary design would probably not require a mapping sentence to be written, as it is artificially simple. I will then offer a series of declarative sentences in which I add another facet in each iteration of the sentence. Again, this procedure is adopted for illustrative purposes, and the researcher would typically not start with a single facet in the mapping sentence and then add successive facets.

An extremely rudimentary example of a declarative mapping sentence for place experience is provided in Figure 2.1. The declarative mapping sentence in this figure presents a template for conducting research into place experience. A single facet is specified and establishes a definition of what constitutes their experience, with elements of social, spatial, service, or aesthetic. The simple sentence is read from left to write as in an ordinary English language sentence. This mapping sentence is read so as to include an element in the reading rather than the facet name. For example, given that there is a single facet (referent) with four elements, there are four possible readings or sentences that can be formed by this declarative mapping sentence:

Person (x) experiences place in terms of the social aspects of the place
Person (x) experiences place in terms of the spatial aspects of the place
Person (x) experiences place in terms of the service aspects of the place
Person (x) experiences place in terms of the aesthetic aspects of the place

In this example, it can be seen that the declarative mapping sentence specifies that there are four possible types of experience that a person may have in any specific place. Furthermore, the declarative mapping sentence requires that the researcher interested in examining the experiences associated with a place design research instruments (observations, questions, and so on) that address the four types of place experience.

	Referent	
	social	
Person (x) experiences the:	spatial	aspects of place.
	service	
	aesthetic	

Figure 2.1 Declarative Mapping Sentence for Place Experience #1

In this initial sentence, the other component is the letter *x*, which specifies the subject of the sentence. It is also the subject of the research that is being conducted. The entity that the letter *x* represents may be very different between studies and may be substituted with a specific individual, a group of individuals, or objects or events when these are the subject of the sentence.

Most mapping sentences are used in situations in which more than a single variable of facet is of interest. Research that has multiple facets with multiple elements (which may also incorporate the effects of background variables) is more likely to be the situation in which a mapping sentence is used. Such complex research presents challenges to the researcher in terms of designing and analysing studies that take into account all of these variables. It is in these cases that the mapping sentence approach comes into its own.

If we return to the example of place experience, the literature would suggest that an individual's understanding of a place does not simply arise through reference to the place in terms of its qualities: its social, service, spatial, and aesthetic aspects. Instead, this facet of referent will interact with other facets (other components of place experience), and these additional variables may be incorporated into the declarative mapping sentence. In Figure 2.2, I have added a facet that focusses on place experience in terms of two elements that specify how central or peripheral a given place experience is for a respondent in terms of achieving his or her purpose in a location. The declarative mapping sentence now reads as follows:

After the first iteration of the declarative mapping sentence (Figure 2.1), I provided all four of the ways in which the declarative mapping sentence may be read. With the inclusion of the focus facet, the possible reading options for the sentence are increased to eight:

> *Person (x) experiences place in terms of the social aspects of the place which are central to his or her purpose in the specified place.*
> *Person (x) experiences place in terms of the spatial aspects of the place which are central to his or her purpose in the specified place.*

	Referent		**Focus**	
Person (x) experiences the:	social spatial service aesthetic	aspects of place, which are:	Central Peripheral	for he or she purpose in the specified palce.

Figure 2.2 Declarative Mapping Sentence for Place Experience #2

Person (x) experiences place in terms of the service aspects of the place which are central to his or her purpose in the specified place.
Person (x) experiences place in terms of the aesthetic aspects of the place which are central to his or her purpose in the specified place.
Person (x) experiences place in terms of the social aspects of the place which are peripheral to his or her purpose in the specified place.
Person (x) experiences place in terms of the spatial aspects of the place which are peripheral to his or her purpose in the specified place.
Person (x) experiences place in terms of the service aspects of the place which are peripheral to his or her purpose in the specified place.
Person (x) experiences place in terms of the aesthetic aspects of the place which are peripheral to his or her purpose in the specified place.

Place experience research has also discovered that the directness of contact is an important feature of our experience of places. I therefore made a change to the declarative mapping sentence for place experience to reflect the potential effects that may occur in purposive experience due to the directness of contact. This is shown in Figure 2.3.

The inclusion of the third facet of level of contact will now be incorporated into research tools that are developed from the mapping sentence. Rather than listing all of the possible questions that arise from the exhaustive combination of the three facets' elements and result in 16 combinations, in the following, I provide a few examples of such combinations:

Person (x) experiences place in terms of the social aspects of the place which are central to his or her purpose and which require direct levels of contact in the specified place.
Person (x) experiences place in terms of the service aspects of the place which are central to his or her purpose and which require indirect levels of contact in the specified place.

	Reference		**Focus**		**Level**	
	social		Central		direct	
Person (x)	spatial	aspects of place,	Peripheral	to he or she purpose,	indirect	levels of contact for their
experiences the:	service	which are:		and which require:		purpose in the specified place.
	aesthetic					

Figure 2.3 Declarative Mapping Sentence for Place Experience #3

Person (x) experiences place in terms of the aesthetic aspects of the place which are peripheral to their purpose and which require indirect levels of contact in the specified place.

Person (x) experiences place in terms of the spatial aspects of the place which are peripheral to their purpose and which require direct levels of contact in the specified place.

I could continue to provide all possible combinations of facet elements, but I believe that the preceding examples demonstrate the process. It should also be noted at this stage that the research tools that arise from combining facet elements – in this example, the questions that may be asked – do not always have to take the somewhat tedious format of my example. For example, the questions do not have to incorporate facets into questions in the same order of the facets in the mapping sentence, and the questions may be re-worded to be less cumbersome whilst still containing the same facet elements.

I have now included the three facets that appear in the literature as being important aspects of people's place experiences. However, the declarative mapping sentence for place experience in Figure 2.3 does not include any background characteristics related to different types of respondents, different places, or other things that may systematically influence how we experience places. Within mapping sentences, these important external influences are taken into account through the inclusion of background facets and their elements. Background facets can be of a number of different types, but their common characteristic is that they have an influence upon the content of the mapping sentence whilst not being a part of that content. An example of this in relation to place experience may be the reason why a person is in a specific location. Possible elements that differentiate users' reasons for being in a place include their being: customers, employees, or visitors to the location. Moreover, the literature, and personal experience, would suggest that people will have a different type of experience and understanding of a place if they are a customer, employee, or visitor. Therefore, a background facet that reflects these types of place users may be included in the declarative mapping sentence.

I have included a single background facet in the declarative mapping sentence in Figure 2.4, but I could have included more background facets. An example of other types of background facets that may be included in research into place experience could be age, gender, or characteristics of the place being viewed, such as retail, industrial, service location, and so on. Background facets sound as if they are somewhat of an afterthought in the design of a mapping sentence, but it is important to note that they may have a major influence in the interpretation of information that arises from a mapping sentence.

	Background		Referent		Focus	
	customer		social		Central	
Person (x)	employee	experiences the:	spatial	aspects of place,	Peripheral	⇨
being a:	visitor		service	which are:		
			aesthetic			

	Level	
to he or she purpose,	direct	levels of contact for their purpose in the specified place.
and which require:	indirect	

Figure 2.4 Declarative Mapping Sentence for Place Experience #4

In Figure 2.4, I provide the example of the declarative mapping sentence for place experience with the inclusion of a background facet.

I have now finished developing a declarative mapping sentence, a research framework which explains the important variables that have been found to influence such experience and how these may be combined to reflect their real-world occurrence. I have also given a few examples of how the declarative mapping sentence may be the basis for the origination of research questions or other tools for the gathering of qualitative data. In the next section of this chapter, I turn from the declarative mapping sentence to the traditional mapping sentence, and I now consider how a declarative mapping sentence may be converted into a traditional mapping sentence in order to collect and analyse quantitative data.

A Traditional Mapping Sentence

I start my consideration of how a traditional mapping sentence is developed by offering a traditional mapping sentence for place experience. This example, given in Figure 2.5, is a modification of the declarative mapping sentence for place experience in Figure 2.4. The only difference in the mapping sentences in Figures 2.4 and 2.5 is that in the latter a response range has been incorporated. The declarative mapping sentence is a specification of a content domain in terms of its important features. The reason for designing a declarative mapping sentence is to clearly specify the important aspects that are believed to structure experience of a particular behavioural or experiential content domain. Qualitative research that uses the declarative mapping sentence is provided with a framework for developing

	Background		Referent		Focus	
	passenger		social		central	
Person (x)	employee	experiences the:	spatial	aspects of place,	peripheral	⇨
being a:	visitor		service	which are:		
			aesthetic			

	Level		Range	
to he or she purpose,	direct	levels of contact with the place,	lesser	
and which require:	indirect	and assesses these to be satisfactory to a:	to	extent
			greater	

Figure 2.5 Traditional Mapping Sentence for Place Experience #5

open-ended enquiries into a research area and given a framework through which to analyse and understand qualitative information or ideas that arise in such research.

The range facet in the present example is a range that runs from lesser to greater extents of satisfaction with a specific place. The response range will be assigned a numerical spread of values from which respondents will chose the number that best represents their satisfaction with the facet element combination that defines their specific experiences of place. For instance, the least extent of satisfaction may be assigned a score of 1, and the greatest extent of satisfaction may be assigned a score of 7, and in this example, a respondent may choose any number from 1 to 7.

One point that should be mentioned is that all types of mapping sentences may be modified by the incorporation of new facets or deletion of existing facets. Mapping sentences may also be amended through the incorporation or the deletion of facet elements in existing facets. Facet elements may be added to an existing facet instead of adding a new facet when the addition of a new facet would lead to a situation in which the content under investigation would be differentiated by the new facet in a way that would result in impossible real-world situations. Having developed either a declarative or traditional mapping sentence for a specific content domain, the researcher has a framework for research in the specified area. The mapping sentence is not a fixed or static framework, but rather it may be adapted and used by researchers to design research into similar or analogous content.

Conclusions

Research into a specified type of behaviour or experience, as illustrated by place experience research, may take either a qualitative or a quantitative form. As well as asking respondents to respond along a numerical range of possibilities, quantitative measurements of a variety of types may be taken. Observations may be made of behaviours and the frequency of such observations noted or the length of their duration recorded, and many other quantitative measurements may be taken. It is also possible to gather qualitative data that reflects a researcher's impressions, interpretations, or observations about a quantitative activity. It can be seen in the descriptions I have provided that mapping sentences are frameworks that allow both qualitative and quantitative analysis of a single study. In such a situation, the mapping sentence structures data gathering and provides a comparable framework for understanding and interpreting the quantitative and qualitative information that arises within a single study.[3]

Psychologists, and other social and behavioural researchers, frequently have to make decisions about the number of variables to include in their research. They may choose to include several variables, which has the potential advantage of being realistic. However, the simultaneous inclusion of multiple variables may make the findings difficult to interpret. Conversely, a single or a limited set of variables may be chosen to allow greater control of the research situation and the more emphatic demonstration of the effects of variables. However, such research is usually less realistic and is less directly generalisable to the real world. I hope that by taking the reader through the process of developing both a declarative and traditional mapping sentence, I have illustrated how the mapping sentence increases the possibility of designing both qualitative and quantitative research that incorporates multiple variables whilst facilitating a clear understanding of complex research domains.

Notes

1. The use of the facet theory approach in general has its foundations in the clear and unambiguous definitions of the research domain provided by the mapping sentence (Alt, 2016).
2. It should be noted that the literature has often supported the notion that people experience places in terms of their purposes in a location, and purposive experience of place will be incorporated in the following example.
3. Indeed, I have used quantitative facet analysis (e.g., Hackett [2013, 2014]) along with the qualitative version of facet analysis and the declarative mapping sentence (Hackett, 2016) to facilitate the understanding of a single research domain (for example, avian behaviour, and aspects of avian behaviour such as blinking whilst asleep and oology Hackett, 2020).

References

Alt, D. (2016) Students' Perceived Constructivist Learning Environment Empirical Examples of the Comparison Between Facet Theory with Smallest Space Analysis and Confirmatory Factor Analysis, *European Journal of Psychological Assessment*, 34(6). https://doi.org/10.1027/1015–5759/a000358.

Borg, I., and Shye, S. (1995) *Facet Theory: Form and Content* (Advanced Quantitative Techniques in the Social Sciences), Thousand Oaks, CA: Sage Publications, Inc.

Canter, D. (1985) How to Be a Facet Researcher, in Canter, D. (ed.) *Facet Theory: Approaches to Social Research*, New York: Springer Verlag, 265–276.

Gurdin, J., Levy, S., and Gratch, H. (1990) The Structure of Social Values, *Contemporary Sociology*, 19(1), 44–46.

Guttman, L. (1947) Scale and Intensity Analysis for Attitude, Opinion and Achievement, in Kelly, G.A. (ed.) *New Methods in Applied Psychology: Proceedings of the Maryland Conference on Military Contributions to Methodology in Applied Psychology Held at the University of Maryland, November 27–28, 1945, Under the Auspices of the Military Division of the American Psychological Association*, College Park, MD: University of Maryland.

Guttman, L. (1954a) A New Approach to Factor Analysis: The Radex, in Lazarsfeld, P.F. (ed.) *Mathematical Thinking in the Social Sciences*, New York: Free Press, 258–348.

Guttman, L. (1954b) An Outline of Some New Methodology for Social Research, *Public Opinion Quarterly*, 18, 395–404.

Guttman, L. (1959a) Introduction to Facet Design and Analysis, in *Proceedings of the Fifteenth International Congress of Psychology, Brussels – 1957*, Amsterdam: North Holland, 130–132.

Guttman, L. (1959b) Introduction to Facet Design and Analysis, *Acta Psychologica*, 15, 130–138.

Guttman, L. (1971) Measurement as Theory, *Psychometrika*, 36, 329–347.

Guttman, R., and Greenbaum, C. (1998) Facet Theory: Its Development and Current Status, *European Psychologist*, 3, 13–36.

Hackett, P.M.W. (2013) *Fine Art and Perceptual Neuroscience: Field of Vision and the Painted Grid, Explorations in Cognitive Psychology Series*, London: Psychology Press.

Hackett, P.M.W. (2014) *Facet Theory and the Mapping Sentence: Evolving Philosophy, Use and Application*, Basingstoke: Palgrave McMillan Publishers.

Hackett. P.M.W. (2016) *Psychology and Philosophy of Abstract Art: Neuroaesthetics, Perception and Comprehension*, Basingstoke: Palgrave McMillan Publishers.

Hackett, P.M.W. (2020) *The Complexity of Bird Behaviour: A Facet Theory Approach*, Cham, CH: Springer.

Maslovaty, N., and Levy, S. (2001) A Comparative Approach in Developing a Structural Value Theory, in Elizur, D. (ed.) *Facet Theory: Integrating Theory Construction with Data Analysis*. Prague, Czech Republic: Karlovy University of Prague, 21–32.

Maslovaty, N., Marshall, A.E., and Alkin, M.C. (2001) Teachers' Perceptions Structured Through Facet Theory: Smallest Space Analysis Versus Factor Analysis, *Educational and Psychological Measurement*, 61, 71–84.

Shirom, A. (1991) *A Facet-theoretic Approach Toward Theorizing in Labor Relations*. Paper Presented at the Third International Facet Theory Conference, Jerusalem, Israel.

3 Declarative Mapping Sentences

Content Summary

Throughout the earlier chapters of this book, I have considered both the declarative and traditional forms of mapping sentences, although I emphasised the traditional form of mapping sentence in the first chapter. In this chapter, I provide more details to support my claims that the declarative mapping sentence may be used with profit and as a trustworthy instrument within qualitative research and philosophical scholarship. In offering further information about the declarative mapping sentence, including some details about its philosophical and linguistic sources, I provide examples of the uses of this approach. The multiple examples I have included in this chapter come from my own research (these include studies I have undertaken in the areas of philosophy and fine art) and from that of other scholars who, in the examples I have chosen, have considered areas as diverse as religious behaviour, the evaluation of IT systems, and clinical reasoning. My aims in this chapter are to argue that by providing clear definitions, in the form of well-structured mereologies that bound and structure a research domain, the declarative mapping sentence may be used to design, conduct, and analyse complex non-numerical research. The examples I provide of research from the literature of the use of mapping sentences in their declarative form support these assertions.

Introduction: Qualitative Research

In the preface and earlier chapters, I have presented both the traditional and declarative versions of the mapping sentence, and the reader should by now be aware that there are many similarities between these two forms of mapping sentences. Examples of such likenesses include that both clearly specify the subjects who will be involved in the research and that both constitute a formal statement of an area of research through the specification of the pertinent aspects or variables (facets) that are of interest within a specific research domain. Furthermore, both declarative and traditional mapping sentences exhaustively describe the facets and their elements within a research domain. Another similarity between the traditional and declarative forms of mapping sentence is that both types also constitute formal propositions about their subject matter, and both involve some sort of input from their research subject(s): that is to say that neither are pure conjecture, although it is possible to use the declarative mapping sentence in a situation where the subject from whom the input is derived is the researcher. In all research in which a mapping sentence is present, the propositional statements that are contained in both types of mapping sentence are interrogated in order to assess the truthfulness or veracity of the structure of the mapping sentence for a research domain.[1]

In this chapter, I will focus on the declarative mapping sentence and its distinguishing features and characteristics along with its use in qualitative research. The strength of qualitative research is the ability of the researcher using such an approach to uncover the meanings that individuals have for and the feelings and thoughts they have towards the content of a particular event, state of affairs, object, and so on. Additionally, qualitative research is able to transmit and communicate these forms of rich and meaningful insight through thick descriptions (Geertz, 1973), which are a specific form of description used in the social sciences and humanities. In these rigorous types of observations of human activities, the researcher documents both the specific phenomenon of interest along with the context of its occurrence. When a researcher develops a thick description, it is usual that he or she will include subjective comments and explanations that arise from the people who are being investigated and described. As well as providing a more complete documentation of the event of interest, thick descriptions include the expressed meanings of those who are associated with the phenomenon, which potentially provides greater understanding for those of us who are reading these descriptions. The ability of qualitative research to facilitate meaningful insight has been noted by many authors, including Gorli et al. (2012), who provided an informative review of qualitative research in the context of multi-method research. In their example, they noted that qualitative research gathered and analysed thick data and developed descriptive information and knowledge. Moreover, because of its idiosyncratic nature, the knowledge that is produced in qualitative research is usually deeply and personally meaningful, which is a strength but which also means that qualitative research findings may be fragmented and disconnected from other research into the same substantive content area. Furthermore, these qualities may result in there being little direct comparability between a project's outcomes and those of previous research that has addressed a similar content area, which has the consequence of retarding the origination of theories about the phenomenon of interest.[2]

These potential weaknesses due to the lack of comparability between qualitative research studies have been among the reasons that have led some social and psychological researchers to favour using a quantitative methodology in their research. Through the use of rigorous sampling procedures in its research design, quantitative research approaches are buttressed by their ability to produce results that may allow researchers to generalise from the findings of their specific project to a broader population (Lincoln and Guba, 1985). Notwithstanding such a strength, concern and criticism have been expressed about quantitative research in regard to its converting human behaviour and experience to numerical indices and in so doing diminishing the richness and personalness of such understanding. Indeed, for this reason, authors such as Townsend et al. (2010) have noted how the understanding produced from quantitative research may fail to result in the development of a useful knowledge base about a subject area. They claim that the conversion of behaviour and experience into numerical indices means the research and its findings become abstracted from reality and the actual experience of those living in the areas the researcher is investigating. Another potential weakness of quantitative research is that the numbers produced in this type of research may also possess a spurious sense of precision and even offer an unwarranted sense of universality that may appear to be a lingua franca that allows communication between different research products.

A familiar example of some of the difficulties associated with using numerical scales when trying to gain meaningful information from an individual can be seen in the question that is often asked by doctors to patients about their pain experiences. Doctors frequently request their patient to respond to the question: "On a scale of one to ten, where one is the least severe and ten is the most, how severe is your pain?" In citing this example, I am not dismissing the clinical usefulness of a response to such a question, but I am warning against a belief that a response to this question would produce a result that is comparable between individuals. For instance, a person who has given birth or who has been involved in a major car accident in which he or she was severely injured may rate the pain he or she is experiencing from a chronic muscle spasm as "4". However, a person who has experienced neither of these two extreme forms of pain and has had little previously experienced acute pain may claim this to be "8 or 9". Furthermore, regardless of previous experience, people differ in terms of how they experience the world and the ways in which they communicate such experiences. In this doctor-patient example, whilst it may be clinically useful to garner such an estimate, the data that this produces should not be seen as comparable to other data, and any form of parametric statistical analyses of the data would be misleading. In this situation, I contend that it is of greater interest to know the person's history and to hear his or her stories and personal experiences, along with his or descriptions of present pain.

Another similar example is provided by Edwards and colleagues (2004). These researchers were interested in individuals' encounters with various techniques in physiotherapy. They noted how respondents were asked about their experiences by being required to provide a number ranging from 0 to 10 (in a manner that was similar to the procedure I stated previously). These authors claimed that this number-based assessment was an abstraction of patients' experiences and that this data did not capture the intricacies of the therapeutic procedure, which lasted several minutes. The authors claimed that by not gathering patients' experiential narratives in regard to the therapeutic intervention that the researchers were metaphorically manipulating pain through the use of a numerical assessment as an indicator variable for gauging success or otherwise of a specific physiotherapy technique.

The previously stated caveats about some of the potential weaknesses in quantitative research are among the reasons that have led me to develop the declarative mapping sentence for use in qualitative research. Throughout this book, I have claimed that the richness of qualitative approaches to research provide peerless levels of understanding, and in this chapter, I emphasise this perspective and note that the declarative mapping sentence forms a flexible template for qualitative research. Furthermore, I suggest that using qualitative research methodologies within the framework of the declarative mapping sentence provides for greater levels of comparability between, and for higher levels of confidence in, qualitative research findings.[3]

In an attempt to justify this bold claim regarding the usefulness of the declarative mapping sentence, I now engage in an exposition regarding the nature of this form of mapping sentence.

When and Why to Use the Declarative Mapping Sentence

When information is interpreted in a reliable manner (in a way that yields similar results when explorations and interpretations of similar content are performed at different times and in different places), such interpretations may be said to possess hermeneutical consistency. During the last decade, I have developed the use of the mapping sentence in non-numerical research. I first used this mapping sentence without specifically distinguishing this from the traditional mapping sentence. Since then, I have called this modified version of the traditional mapping sentence the declarative mapping sentence (Greggor and Hackett, 2018; Hackett, 2019a, b, 2018c, 2017a, b, c, 2016a, b, 2015, 2014a, b, 2013, 1983; Hackett et al., 2018, 2016, 2011; Koval et al., 2016; Lou and Hackett, 2018; Schwarzenbach and Hackett, 2015; Shkoler et al., 2020). My reason for developing the declarative mapping sentence has been to attempt to provide a framework that is both theoretically and empirically valid for designing and interpreting qualitative research. I have undertaken my research into the declarative mapping sentence in terms of this being a generic structural ontology that offers the potential to yield hermeneutically consistent findings. The declarative mapping sentence is able to achieve this consistency through the structure of its ontological components and the mereological relationships between these whilst allowing the content of an enquiry to be idiosyncratic and determined by the participant.

In this chapter, I pursue attempts to justify this claim by tracing the declarative nature of this research instrument from its metaphysical and linguistic sources. I also provide examples of declarative mapping sentences which I and other researchers have used to address issues in the social sciences and humanities. I make the argument for the general structure of a sentence as being suitable for embodying and designing complex research that is clearly defined and bounded by the sentence's structure. The declarative mapping sentence may also be called or thought of as a declarative mapping or a declarative mapping statement, a propositional mapping, or a mapping statement. These different terms lay emphasis upon the slightly different functions a declarative mapping sentence may perform in qualitative enquiry, and other phrases may be employed to describe the particular way in which a declarative mapping sentence is used in any particular research study. The declarative mapping sentence is a sophisticated tool for use in qualitative research.[4] In order to develop the declarative mapping sentence, my research has employed facet theory in the sense that I described earlier when I spoke of this as being a philosophical approach toward research content (Hackett, 2013, 2014a, 2016b).

I have provided some background information to the development of the declarative mapping sentence, and I now provide some examples of the ways in which I have used this research approach. For example, an area of a highly subjective/qualitative human experience within which I have extended the use of a mapping sentence is the perception and understanding of various types of abstract fine art (Hackett, 2016a, 2017c).

Abstract Fine Art

Paul Crowther is a philosopher whose work has been on the philosophy and the history of art. In *Defining Art: Creating the Canon* (Crowther, 2007), he considers the values of an aesthetic orientation[5] when it comes to defining art. He attempts to answer questions such as what constitutes art, what accords value to an artwork, and what are the criteria for evaluating the merits of a work of art? Crowther takes on and extends a phenomenological perspective, emphasising fundamental aspects of human perception, and applies this to visual art addressing both abstract and conceptual fine art.

Crowther also questions the idea that artistic value is a product of aesthetics. Instead, he includes in his model of perception such characteristics within a piece of art as imitation and representation. He also stresses the somewhat ethereal links among such features as artistic value, imitation, knowledge, a person's understanding of the perhaps hidden historical links with a piece of art, and the work's connexions to the art canon. An important component of his understanding is the notion of an image's style, which he says facilitates the deciphering of a work's thematic topic and through which artistic merit may arise from an originality of style.[6]

An artwork's value in the 20th century, according to Crowther, has been reduced, has deteriorated, or has been dismissed because of the rise of consumerism during the post-modern age. Social and economic fashions have come to determine artistic value, and the significance of the creation of an artwork is downgraded behind a person's experiences with an art occurrence or an object that we call art.

I first employed Paul Crowther's writing in my research into the perception of two-dimensional abstract fine art (Hackett, 2016b). In essence, Crowther offers an ontological structure for the experiential processes associated with our encounters with abstract art, and I incorporated his work as the basis for my own research. I took Crowther's ontology and adapted this in my evaluation and analysis of abstract three-dimensional art. Furthermore, for Crowther (2007), the phenomenological experience of three-dimensional abstraction is cardinal, as are what he calls the complex contextual qualities of visual space as a location where we come to understand our immediate visual perceptions. Moreover, Crowther states that if we did not occupy a contextual visual space, our perceptions would only exist in two flat dimensions.

When considering an abstract artwork, Crowther posits eight defining dimensions, which he says may be combined and/or sub-divided, to exhaustively account for all such artwork. His dimensions are 1) an artwork's resemblance to particular visual forms and amalgamations of colours, shapes, and textures (e.g., seeing patterns in waves or clouds); 2) the elicitation of psychological conditions that come about through a visual form's gestural associations (e.g., shapes that we feel are violent or aggressive or colours we feel to be depressing); 3) our awareness of features, relations, or states of affairs within our vision (e.g., minute features on an object's surface, the configuration of features within an object: novel perspectives, brief atmospheric effects, and so on); 4) events, items, and states of affairs that can potentially exist in novel perceptual and physical environments; 5) visual arrangements that are brought about when common events, items, and states of affairs are reconfigured, destroyed, deconstructed, reduced, reconstructed, varied, and so on; 6) visual marks or copies of existing, future, or counterfactual events, items, and states of affairs; 7) spatial and structural features, such as colour, volume, shape, texture, density, geometric structure, changes in positions, and being alone or in various combinations; and 8) experiences and events that are imaginary or dreamlike.

Crowther's eight dimensions form a thorough and comprehensive listing of perceptual characteristics of art abstraction, and in my earlier writing (Hackett, 2016b), I provided a summary of Crowther's dimensions, which I repeat here, as it offers a succinct account of his dimensions:

1) **resemblances** – creating resemblances through combination
2) **gestural associations** – evocation through gestural associations with visual forms
3) **revelations** of usually invisible visual features
4) **novel environments** – existence as a product of usual environments
5) **neoteric configurations** – reconfiguration of the familiar producing neoteric visual configurations
6) **visual suggestions** – visual traces or suggestions
7) **spatiality/structure** – structural features of spatial appearances
8) **fantasy** – imaginary and dream phenomena

Crowther suggests that his model stipulates a theoretical structure which facilitates a greater understanding of abstract art. I questioned Crowther's model in terms of its adequacy in demonstrating "ongoing reciprocal interaction or influence that must exist between different characteristics of such a complex experience as is involved in perceiving, understanding and appreciating, valuing, disliking, etc., of an artwork" (Hackett, 2016b, p. 42). In an attempt to address what I saw as the shortcomings in Crowther's model, I developed a mapping sentence to depict the perception of abstract three-dimensional fine art (Figure 3.1) which is sympathetic to the interactions that exist between Crowther's eight characteristics. My declarative mapping sentence model provides a framework within which his ontology may be assembled, combined, or aggregated. My declarative mapping sentence adds to and builds upon Crowther's dimensions and offers an explicit inter-dimensional phenomenological mereology of these characteristics.

This declarative mapping sentence for three-dimensional abstract fine art grew out of not only Crowther's ontology but also my earlier research and mapping sentence for two-dimensional abstract art (Hackett, 2016b). This earlier mapping sentence provided a template to enable the identification of

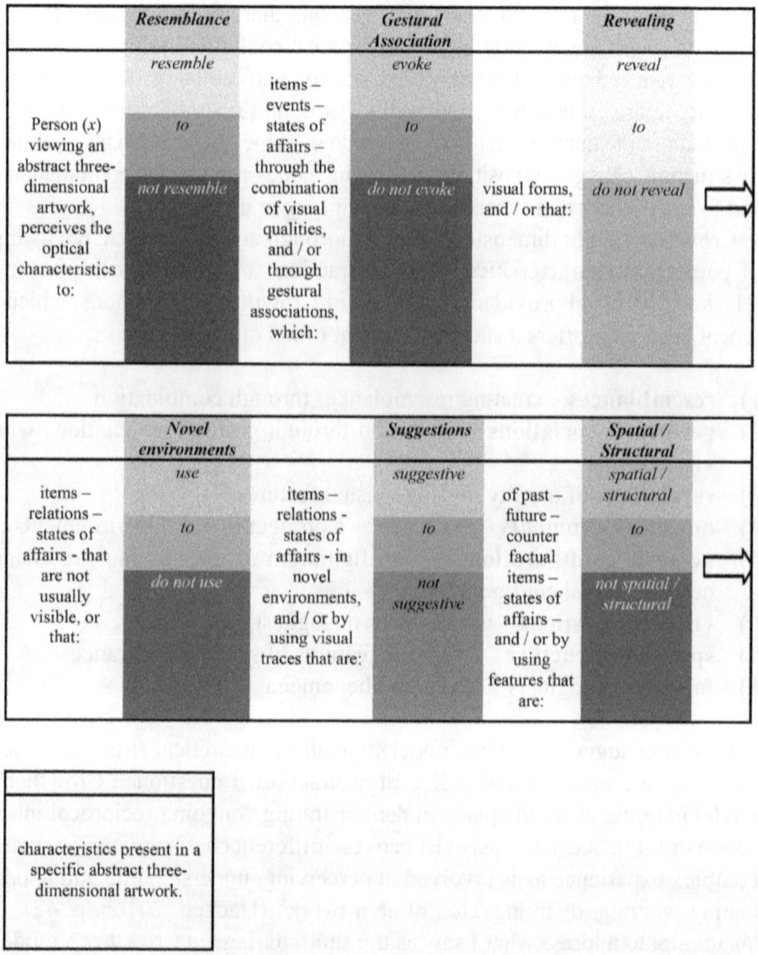

Figure 3.1 Declarative Mapping Sentence for Understanding the Experience of Perceiving Abstract Art

Source: Adapted from Hackett (2017c), p. 88.

how any specific two-dimensional abstract fine art pieces may differ from other two-dimensional abstract artworks. The present declarative mapping sentence extends such discrimination to the realm of three-dimensional art. Furthermore, by using partial order scalogram analysis, I was also able to show how some of Crowther's eight characteristics did not seem to be as important in their capacity of offering an account of experiences of abstract three-dimensional art as were other characteristics.

Aristotle's Categories

Having demonstrated how I have used a declarative mapping sentence to investigate the area of abstract three-dimensional fine art, I next turn my attention very briefly to another example of my use of the declarative mapping sentence. In this research, I was concerned with attempting to provide a phenomenological account of Aristotle's categories (Aristotle et al., 1938). I have presented this depiction of Aristotle's categories in my earlier writing (Hackett, 2014a), and my reason to include this declarative mapping sentence here is to provides an illustrative example of the application of the declarative mapping sentence in a philosophical enquiry. This example of the application of the declarative mapping sentence is given in Figure 3.2.

It has been my experience that developing a declarative mapping sentence for a content domain often enables me to better appreciate the complexity

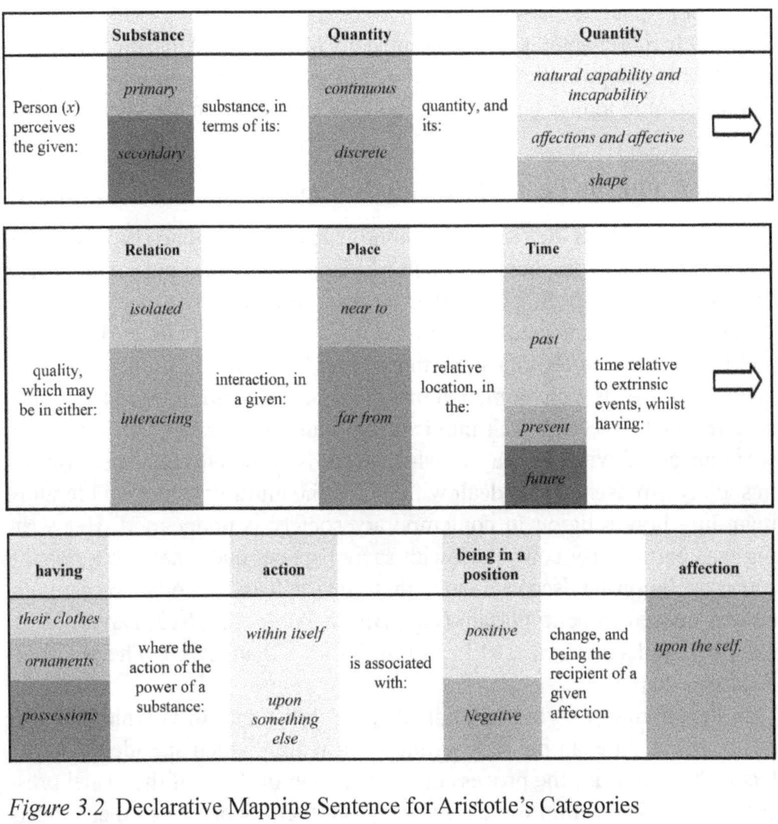

Figure 3.2 Declarative Mapping Sentence for Aristotle's Categories

Source: (adapted from Hackett, 2014a)

of the content in which I have an interest. Furthermore, the depiction of an area of interest in a declarative mapping sentence format may reveal or suggest possibilities in terms of the interconnections between the sub-components of the domain in an unrivalled manner. In Figure 3.6, the presentation of Aristotle's categories in a declarative mapping sentence form not only clearly specifies Aristotle's ten different ontological categories but also suggests and proposes a possible manner in which the categories may be combined and may be understood to exist as a phenomenological and complete whole. On the understanding contained in the declarative mapping sentence for Aristotle's categories, the components of his ontology are portrayed with connective language that joins the categories that take the form of facets with possible elements. This is an initial mapping sentence that raises questions about Aristotle's ontology and suggests a starting point for research into the phenomenological instantiation of the categories. Future research could be conducted to modify the mapping sentence and to suggest different arrangements and connective links between the facets of categories and their respective elements.

So far in this chapter, I have presented my own research that has employed a declarative mapping sentence, and in the next sections, I provide examples of the use of mapping sentences in their declarative form by other scholars.

Religion and the Process of Sacralisation

Another example of the use of a declarative mapping sentence is provided in the research of geographer Lucyna Przybylska (2014). Przybylska's research was concerned with the period that followed the time when the social sciences incorporated a secular paradigm, focusing on scholars in the U.S.A. and Europe. She notes that since then these disciplines have started to discuss religiosity as a phenomenon that merits consideration, as it constitutes an important aspect of both public and private life. Przybylska's research was concerned with the way in which what is essentially a resacralisation in society is present and is dealt with within the multi-disciplinary literature regarding how religion in contemporary society is understood. Her writing was particularly concerned with sacred spaces and what she terms the society-religion-landscape themes that geographers and other researchers have proposed to be important (e.g., Bilska-Wodecka, 2012; Davie, 2013; Havlíček and Hupková, 2013; Klima, 2011; Sołjan, 2012; Theije, 2012; Zelinsky, 2010).

In her writing, Przybylska addresses the Polish city of Gdynia and proposes this as an example of a setting from within which she identifies the facets that comprise the process of sacralisation in terms of the visual presence of religion within the city. Przybylska then incorporates these facets into a declarative mapping sentence (Figure 3.3), which she claims to be a detailed scheme for the representation of this visual religious phenomenon. Przybylska describes the facets she incorporated into the declarative mapping sentence and employs several qualitative approaches to research to investigate these including field observation, analysis of source documents, analysis and criticism of the bibliography, visual documentation, and participant observation.

Throughout her research and writing about her results, Przybylska used the declarative mapping sentence both as a guide to her research and her research write-up and as a frame for interpreting her results. She claims that the declarative mapping sentence she used "illustrates a kind of model that emphasises different components of the term landscape sacralisation, (and) it can be used to interpret, step by step, the complex phenomenon of visual manifestation of religion in the landscape" (Przybylska, 2014, p. 118). She continues to say that the declarative mapping sentence provides a definition of the phenomenon of sacralisation and also facilitates the exploration of the facets in the sentence which provides for comprehensive research to be conducted characteristic of the facets and elements in the sentence.

Przybylska applies the multidimensional structure of the declarative mapping sentence to understand sacralisation as this applied within the city

A1
Religious (erecting sacred sites and symbols)
(sharing faith)

A2
other needs (aesthetic)
(symbolic domains)
(sharing experience)

B
As well as (politically)
(economically)
(demographically)
(culturally)
(environmentally)

determined *Home religious* ability of expression in a

C
(private) way
(group)
(institutional)

D
Influence (architectural)
(nominative)
(temporal)

E
sacralisation of (urban/non-urban) public spaces
– city, town, village
– street, road, trail
– hill, mountain

F
leading to (old) forms related to the sacred
(new)

Figure 3.3 A Mapping Sentence of the Process of Sacralisation (Przybylska, 2014, p. 118)

of Gdynia. The sentence's structure enabled her to focus her attention on either the different types of needs that people had (A1, A2) or possibilities of *Homo religious* (B) when people expressed their faith in public spaces. It was also possible for her to direct her attention towards visual forms of sacralisation, which she sub-divided into collective and individual forms of expression (C), aspects of sacralisation (D), and early and modern forms of the sacred (F) as these related to various spatial units (E).

Przybylska concluded that the declarative mapping sentence was useful "when describing determinants, aspects and forms of sacralisation. It enables a step by step exploration of different facets of the multidimensional process of landscape sacralisation" (Przybylska, 2014, p. 131). Her research, she claimed, has demonstrated that stating a declarative mapping sentence allowed for either each individual facet to be focussed upon in research or for numerous facets to be incorporated together at a stage of an enquiry that allowed a more comprehensive form of research. Furthermore, she believed that her declarative mapping sentence of sacralisation offered a unique conceptualisation of this process in an original format within the geography of religion literature.

Characteristics of the Clinical Reasoning Process

A further and slightly different use of a declarative mapping sentence is provided in the work of Jonas Wihlborg and colleagues (2019) which investigated the competence and education of ambulance nurses. Their research employed a qualitative research approach which they also later quantitatively coded. Consequently and unusually for a declarative mapping sentence, a range facet is present which comprises the two elements of analytical and non-analytical. However, the researchers called this an organisation range rather than a response range. This facet allowed the information that was gathered in the qualitative research to be stringently organised rather than requiring respondents to provide a response from one of these two range values. As such, they did not gather responses from respondents, and the mapping sentence is declarative rather than traditional (Figure 3.4).

Wihlborg et al. (2019) stated an overall research question that was "what similarities, differences and characteristics of clinical reasoning are found among groups of specialist ambulance nurse students and professional specialist ambulance nurses?" (Wihlborg, et al., p 49). To investigate this question, a study was conducted in Sweden, a country where all ambulances are staffed with a qualified registered nurse who has specialist 40-week ambulance nurse education and clinical practice. Whilst training, students possess varying levels of clinical nursing and ambulance care experience. Those included in the study were either attending or had attended specialist

Facet A – Clinical reasoning process

Groups reasoning (x) about
- a1. Considering patient situation
- a2. Collecting information
- a3. Processing information
- a4. Identifying problems
- a5. Establishing goals
- a6. Taking action
- a7. Evaluating outcome
- a8. Reflecting and processing

Facet B – Case content

focusing on
- b1. Nursing
- b2. Medicine
- b3. Ethics
- b4. Legislation
- b5. Organisation

Range

is characterised by
- r1. An analytical
- r2. A non-analytical

approach

Figure 3.4 Mapping Sentence Used to Explore the Characteristics of the Clinical Reasoning Process (Wihlborg et al., 2019, p. 49)

ambulance nurse training. Participants (n=32) were composed of 19 students and 13 specialist ambulance nurses who were allocated to case discussion groups.

A case study method (Kim et al., 2006; Mauffette-Leenders et al., 2005) was employed within which written narrative case stories were given to the groups to discuss. Those taking part were familiar with the case study method as a form of teaching. Participants were all actively engaged in the discussions that lasted from half an hour to almost an hour and a half. Open discussions involved the researcher listening actively but only interrupting and interacting with participants occasionally in order to clarify points. The researchers designed two case scenarios for discussion that both included a broad content spectrum which provided the chance to focus on multiple aspects of the ambulance service's clinical work. There was also a wide variety of features for the groups to discuss which were relevant to both their theoretical education and their professional practice. A template was used which provided a framework for discussions that included facts, problems, analysis, action, predictions, and outcome. A second observer was present and took notes of group engagement and dynamics, verbal and non-verbal communication, and group interactivity. The timed and recorded group discussions were transcribed verbatim prior to analysis.

The declarative mapping sentence that was used to design the study was also employed to analyse transcripts. In their mapping sentence, the authors included the two content facets of A, clinical reasoning and B, case content. In facet A (clinical reasoning), there were elements of a1, considering the patient situation; a2, collecting information; a3, processing information; a4, identifying problems; a5, establishing goals; a6, taking action; a7, evaluating outcomes; and a8, reflecting and processing. These elements were derived from the principles of the clinical reasoning process as stated by Levett-Jones et al. (2010). Wihlborg et al. (2019) note that they derived the facet elements directly from this model of the types of reasoning that occur in a clinical setting. Furthermore, they said that by sub-dividing reasoning in this way, they were able to reveal the components of the clinical process that respondents primarily reasoned about.

Facet B was called case content and was made up of five elements: b1, nursing; b2, medicine; b3, ethics; b4, legislation; and b5, organisation. The case content facet, the authors claimed, enabled them to sort reasoning units by the setting of respondents' reasoning. The first element of this facet represented the central aspects of nursing, including communication, relationships, and environmental considerations representing a holistic nursing approach (Ekman et al., 2011; Henderson, 1991). The second element, b2, represented physical status, pathophysiology, and pharmaceutical treatment or diagnoses. The other three elements embodied features that were associated with respondents' reasoning.

The range facet in the declarative mapping sentence was dichotomous with elemental values of r1, an analytical approach, or r2, a non-analytical approach. These two types of reasoning were derived from published descriptions of clinical reasoning (Durning et al., 2015; Eva, 2005; Marcum, 2012). The researchers assigned each of the units of reasoning to one of either r1 or r2 depending upon the depth of knowledge that respondents used when completing that item within the groups' discussions. Assigning a quantitative value allowed them to turn their qualitative information into quantitative data. They analysed this data and produced a three-dimensional figure to represent relationships in the data broken down by facets and their elements.

The results from these analyses demonstrated that the declarative mapping sentence was appropriate and able to provide a framework for analysis of the reasoning in all respondent groups. The authors were also able to identify many characteristics of reasoning in general and different patterns of reasoning elements between respondent groups. For example, one of the student groups alternated between analytical and non-analytical reasoning irrespective of content or process. They discovered this group became moderately more analytical when reasoning about nursing and medicine, which was a major component of their reasoning. The group focused on medicine and nursing with less concentration on ethics and legislation. A small amount of the group's reasoning focussed on collecting information, and they hardly ever focussed on reflection and processing. The second student group displayed a pattern of analytical and non-analytical reasoning with most reasoning being about nursing. A large amount of this group's reasoning was about organisation and medicine, with little about legislation. All elements of facet A were subject to this group's reasoning, but they infrequently reasoned about collecting information, reflecting, and processing. The group of professional ambulance nurses primarily employed non-analytical reasoning, especially in reference to the evaluation of nursing. However, the authors noted that that analytical reasoning was present within both facets. Ethics and legislation received the smallest amount of discussion, and collecting information received less discussion than evaluation, reflecting, and processing. Professional reasoning addressed nearly all elements of content and process facets and nearly all facet combinations. Some practices were common among all groups, such as focussing most on evaluation and least on collecting information with a large part being about ethics and less about legislation. Students usually used analytical reasoning and processed information more than professionals.

To conclude, Wihlborg et al. (2019) stated that during the case discussions, professionals appeared to be influenced by their experiences and reflectivity in terms of the content and the process of the clinical reasoning. These specialist nurses mainly employed non-analytical approaches whilst students, who had less experience of practical nursing, typically used an analytical reasoning process.

Wihlborg et al.'s (2019) research is of particular interest in the context of this book, as their research was conducted within a declarative mapping sentence and patterns of activities were distinguished using this framework. The researchers were also able to distinguish between students and trained nurses in terms of the facets and elements in the declarative mapping sentence. It is also worthy of note that this research represents a blending of qualitative research and a subsequent quantitative transformation and analysis.

In the next section, I will be presenting research that investigates the theoretical basis of facet theory and mapping sentences. The research was conducted by Zhang et al. (2016), who looked into the importance of establishing clear and well-defined constructs when investigating a content area. As well as considering the theoretical underpinnings of research, the authors address the application of research into users' reactions to information technology.

Using Information Technology

According to the American Psychological Association, positivism is "a family of philosophical positions holding that all meaningful propositions must be reducible to sensory experience and observation and thus that all genuine knowledge is to be built on strict adherence to empirical methods of verification" (APA, 2020a). Moreover, positivism rejects that truth may be established through speculative philosophy, religion, and so on and promotes scientific procedure and empirical methods as being the framework within which valid forms of investigation should be conducted (APA, 2020a). Conversely, the constructivist position holds that individuals are active in constructing their perceptions of the objects, events, states of affairs, and so on that are around them. We perceive, interpret, and understand the world of our senses, say constructivists, through reference to our existing knowledge and experiences (APA, 2020b). When taking a positivist view of the world, a researcher is looking for replicable results that tell of causality. The world, on this understanding, is a predictable place with commonalities in our existence. However, for those who would adopt a constructivist approach to their encounters with the world, meaning and understanding are inherently individualistic and in a constant state of construction and re-construction.

Zhang and colleagues (2016) note the distinction between adopting either a constructivist or positivist perspective and comment upon how this will be associated with choosing to use specific and different approaches to research. Specifically, the authors relate the preceding two orientations to their consideration of facet theory as a methodology. They intentionally and explicitly couch their writing from a position they see as midway between a constructivist and positivist position, or, as they say, a neutral stance is adopted. Zhang and colleagues' position on the positivist-constructivist dimension, as with all other researchers' positivist-constructivist philosophical orientation, is not just an interesting feature but has a large effect upon the type and extent of clarity we expect the constructs we investigate to have. This is also true of what a researcher expects from a research design and the conceptual underpinnings of such a strategy. An example of how a person's stance on the positivist-constructivist dimension is how this influences the use of a mapping sentence. If the researchers are from a positivist tradition, they may demand or at least expect the constructs they use to predict their observations to do exactly this: predict observations. It is also probable that they expect this predictive relationship to hold true in different research situations. In contrast, a researcher adopting a constructivist stance may, as Zhang et al. (2016) put it, "develop constructs merely to label particular phenomena within a context . . . and hence, might not hold the same view on construct clarity as positivist researchers" (p 9). Furthermore, these authors note how constructivists may typically not expect or desire that their constructs possess the ability to be readily operationalised for employment in different situations.

From this neutral stance, the paper by Zhang and colleagues (2016) focusses on and argues for the essential criterion of construct clarity in evaluating conceptualisation. Gruber (1993) defines *conceptualisation* as "an abstract, simplified view of the world that we wish to represent for some purpose" (Gruber, 1993, p. 199), where conceptualisations inform a variety of ontologies, each of which has its own language and set of ontological commitments. In their writing, they acknowledge that a construct and a concept are different entities but that within the literature, they have been used synonymously, and they adopt this practice. Their research is concerned with theory development and more precisely with the consideration of conceptualisation in this developmental process. The researchers come from the discipline of information technology (IT), and they make reference to IT in their writing.

I am spending time considering the work of Zhang et al. (2016), as they are concerned with and emphasise their belief that facet theory's central value lies in its implied login, rather than the typical use of facet theory as reported in the literature, which emphasises quantitative measurement and techniques for empirical analysis (McGrath, 1968, 1984; Lange, 2008). Zhang et al. concentrate upon construct clarity and its role in conceptualisation. According to the authors, constructs are the bricks from which theories are constructed, and they cite Weber (2012) in support of this claim. Constructs are formulated by researchers who use conceptualisations in order to delineate abstract concepts that are associated with a given phenomenon (Kaplan, 1964) and where conceptualisation specifies the constructs' meaning (Schwab, 1980). Given the frequently stressed importance of constructs, this means there is an imperative for appropriate conceptualisation.

Central to Zhang et al.'s paper is the logic of what they call facet theory methodology, which provides assistance for clarifying the conceptualisation of constructs. They state that when attempting to achieve clarification in our understanding of concepts, it is important to initially consider criteria, such as the comparability of concepts, whilst considering how constructs may be contrasted. Additionally, they state the importance of establishing a clear and explicit basis for the comparison and contrast of constructs.

In attempting to establish construct clarity, the researcher must, they say, rely on a fundamental belief system, a process which Kaplan (1964) observed is prone to infinite regression. However, Zhang et al. take a practical and realistic approach of the sort advocated by Van de Ven (2007), and they accept that semantic and constitutive definitions, whilst attempting to unambiguously delineate a concept's meaning and usage, must remain in some ways equivocal. However, as Van der Ven continues, researchers with a specific area of concern will likely need to establish a level of tolerance for an acceptable degree of uncertainty in their study. Zhang et al. (2016) further claim that the logical foundations of a facet theory methodology provide a visualisation of the ways in which concepts should relate to each other and impel the researcher towards the clarification of their concepts.

Zhang and colleagues conducted their research in order to instigate what they saw to be the cardinal importance of conceptualisation. They also identified the importance of concomitant issues of the comparability of findings from different research projects and the ability, or lack thereof, of such findings to contribute in a cumulative manner to the development of knowledge. They couched their exposition and writing within the realm of IT literature on value in order to demonstrate the importance of clear definitions of the constructs being used in a research project and to emphasise the relevance of construct clarity within IT. They noted that whilst there is a literature on construct validity and ways of establishing this (e.g., MacKenzie et al., 2011; Petter et al., 2007; Straub et al., 2004; Suddaby, 2010), less has been written on construct clarity and strategies to achieve clear conceptualisation.[7] Openly and unambiguously defined constructs also permit a clear understanding of what falls within a research domain of interest (Weber, 2012).

Zhang et al. (2016) stressed the importance, when attempting to achieve concept clarity, of removing confusion about how constructs relate to one another and proposed two ways of attempting to achieve this. First, they proposed that this is achieved through semantic definitions (in which the meaning of a term is described through reference to its similarities and differences with other terms)[8] and constitutive definitions (a definition achieved through explaining a concept through allusion to the parts of which it is composed) (Van de Ven, 2007). In their attempt to investigate construct clarity in conceptualisation, Zhang et al. (2016) review the principles of facet theory (Guttman, 1954a, b), which they take from McGrath (1968). They cite Guttman (1971) as claiming he developed facet theory to counter the capricious nature of definitions in which words may be used to mean what the researcher requires. Guttman goes on to recommend a reliable formation of a concept which entails stating the central concept along with other concepts that possess common meaning within a definitional framework which constitutes the content universe for the domain of interest. Guttman is ostensibly defining a declarative mapping sentence, which is what Zhang and colleagues (2016) used in their exploration of construct clarity and how facet theory was able to achieve such clarity through its categorial definitions of concepts. An illustrative example of a declarative mapping sentence they produced is shown in Figure 3.5. This sentence describes performance on an intelligence test and was an adaptation of the mapping sentence for intelligence produced by Guttman and Greenbaum (1998, p. 161).

Facet theory, according to (Guttman and Greenbaum, 1998) was originated so as to offer a systematic way of developing theories about human behaviour, as well as facilitating the designing of research projects and analysing the resulting data. In the mapping sentence in Figure 3.5, the first facet (A) states ways in which a person may respond to an orally presented intelligence. This facet states that there are three ways in which a response may be made: oral expression, manual manipulation expression, or paper and pencil expression. The second facet (B) specifies the types of language through which the person being tested may communicate his or her response (verbal, numerical, or geometric). The third facet (C) is the type of intelligence-related ability that the person has to employ (inference, application, or learning). It is obvious that if a researcher who is interested in understanding the performance on intelligence tests refers to the preceding declarative mapping sentence, he or she will be able to clearly understand the responses given by someone completing the test and also will be able to compare the performance of different test takers. With this description of the manner in which a declarative mapping sentence may be used, let us consider Zhang and his colleagues' research.

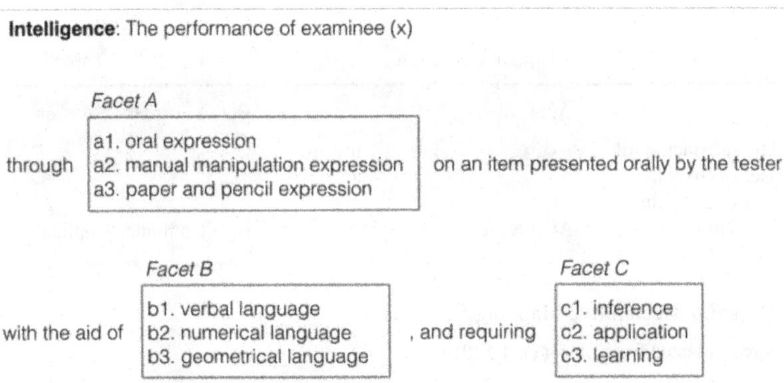

Figure 3.5 Declarative Mapping Sentence for Intelligence (Zhang et al. (2016, p. 7)

It is with a degree of aplomb that Zhang et al. (2016) use a declarative rendition of a mapping sentence to explore conceptual items that cover the area of IT users' satisfaction. They note how three concepts related to satisfaction within the area of IT have been identified: user satisfaction (Wixom and Todd, 2005), user information satisfaction (Ives et al., 1983), and end-user computing satisfaction (Doll and Torkzadeh, 1988). The three forms of satisfaction are specified as the first facet (the facet of target) of their enquiry, as they all address the notion of an evaluation of a specific target, which is the focus of participants' satisfaction. They also noted how there are two ways in which a person can express a reaction to IT, and that is through stating an attitude or a belief, and they stated this in their second facet. These two facets[9] constituted a definitional framework and a clear specification of their conceptualisation and their use of the construct of satisfaction in relation to IT. They tabulated the content of this domain in the following way:

Table 3.1 An Example of Facets

Facet	*User Satisfaction*	*User Information Satisfaction*	*End-User Computing Satisfaction*
A: Evaluative Response	A[1]: Attitude	A[2]: Belief	A[1]: Attitude
B: Evaluative Target	B[1]: Information System	B[1]: Information System	B[2]: Computer Application

The preceding table, Table 3.1, tabulates the content of a declarative mapping sentence but without connective words and phrases. In Figure 3.6, I have re-formatted their table as a declarative mapping sentence:

	Facet A Evaluative Response		Facet B Evaluative Target
The satisfaction of user (x) may be characterised in terms of his or her:	A(1) Attitude	towards a:	B(1) Information System
	A(2) Belief		B(2) Computer Application

Figure 3.6 Declarative Mapping Sentence

Source: Adapted from Zhang et al. (2016).

Under the logic in Figure 3.6 and Table 3.1, Zhang and colleagues (2016) were able to characterise user satisfaction with IT through the combination of elements A[1]B[1] user information satisfaction as A[2]B[1] and end-user computing satisfaction as A[1]B[2].[10] They continue by noting how when defining a domain using a facet theory approach, the researcher uses a mapping sentence (Shye, 1994; Hackett, 2014; Levy, 1990), and if this is well designed, then all of the concepts that fall into that domain that will be characterised by an element profile.

Reference to Zhang, et al.'s (2106) writing demonstrates that the declarative use of the mapping sentence also fulfils the initial aim for facet theory (as articulated by Louis Guttman, 1954a), as it allows a rigorous and methodical way through which to formulate hypotheses and theories within a complex research area that possesses multiple variables in its design. Guttman stated that in order to develop a theory, it is important to start by stating a definitional framework for the domain of interest and then conduct enquiries to ascertain whether there is empirical evidence to support or refute this structure. In facet theory, it is the mapping sentence that provides the definition and the framework within which correspondence is investigated.

When considering the value of a classification system, such as that provided by the declarative mapping sentence, criteria are needed against which the system may be assessed. McGrath (1968) put forward seven requirements that a system of classification must meet and Zhang et al. (2016) modified the seven principles or requirements. Zhang and colleagues' principles are as follows:

1. Concepts in a content universe should be specified in terms of all relevant facets.
2. The facets, collectively, should be logically exhaustive of the content universe.
3. The logical relationships among facets should be specified; independence among facets is preferred.
4. Each facet should be analysed into a set of collectively exhaustive elements.
5. Each facet should be analysed into a set of mutually exclusive elements.
6. The logical relationships among elements of a facet should be specified.
7. The relationships among the concepts defined according to the facets and the elements of facets should correspond to the focal phenomenon.

(Zhang et al., 2016, p. 9)

The preceding principles were developed by McGrath (1968) in reference to a literature that comprised traditional mapping sentences used in quantitative research. However, the requirements stated by both McGrath and Zhang et al. apply to any system of classification, and therefore, they are directly relevant to the declarative mapping sentence. It is also apparent that the declarative mapping sentence fulfils the requirements of a valuable approach to classification.

I developed the declarative mapping sentence in order to provide a flexible and situationally responsive framework within which to conduct qualitative and philosophical inquiries. Zhang et al. (2016) are clear that researchers who adopt either a positivist or constructivist position may expect rather different things in regard to the clarity of the definitions of their constructs. They provide the examples that a positivist researcher may stipulate that a construct is able to predict the empirical observations that they make and that constructs are transferable across research settings. The opposite position would likely be assumed by researchers working within a constructivist framework in terms of their constructs' abilities of prediction and transferability. The declarative mapping sentence operates primarily within a constructivist worldview and is in accordance with what Zhang et al. (2016) term *the principle of concordance or contiguity*, as the declarative mapping sentence is able to accommodate diverse views. They emphasised their belief that there is no need to "constrain the target concepts to those emphasizing empirical prediction; instead, (it may be used) for concepts that do not emphasize strong empirical prediction or 'mirroring reality'" (p 11). The sort of concepts they are thinking of here include philosophical, incorporeal, or linguistic concepts, such as "'dilemma', 'paradox', 'system', 'adaptation', and 'punctuated equilibrium'" (p 11). The role of their declarative form of mapping sentence is to enable a scholar to determine a sentence's definitional framework in relation to an "interpreted or constructed phenomenon" (p 11). Moreover, Zhang et al. (2016) state that a mapping sentence's utility may be established through the repeated and continuous use of the concepts by researchers.

In this chapter, I have presented my own research and that of other scholars who have employed or investigated the use of a declarative mapping sentence. This very brief review has, I believe, suggested that there is utility in using this form of sentence in the design and interpretation of qualitative research into complex events. In the remainder of this chapter, I will reflect upon some final theoretical considerations and characteristics associated with the declarative mapping sentence.

Reflections on the Range Facet

Having demonstrated the use of the declarative mapping sentence, I believe that at this point, it will be helpful to recap the use of this research device. A declarative mapping sentence is composed of the following components and characteristics:

- specification of the person who is the focus of the sentence, is the subject of the research, or is reading, understanding, or in some way responding to the declarative mapping sentence
- background facet list characteristics that are not a component of the research domain but necessary to understand the domain or are at least influential in the instantiation of the mapping sentence ontology
- specification of a mapping sentence ontology through both a content ontology (selected sub-divisions of the ontology as facets and facet elements) and a connective ontology (words and phrases connecting facets and facet elements)
- an explicit statement of the nature of extant relationships within the mapping sentence ontology in part-to-part (facet / facet element to facet / facet element) or part-to-whole (facet / facet element to mapping sentence) terms

It should be noted that the declarative mapping sentence in Figure 3.6, and in nearly all of the other examples of declarative mapping sentences I have provided, lacks a range facet, which is cardinal to the traditional mapping sentence. The absence of a range facet is an extremely important aspect of the declarative form of the mapping sentence. In the traditional mapping sentence, the range facet is one of the tool's great strengths. This strength is due to the way the range focusses and defines the type and the meaning of the measurements that the research defined by the mapping sentence will make and thus ensures consistency. The absence of the range facet in the declarative form of the sentence is due to the more open-ended types of observations undertaken in qualitative enquiries. Not having a range facet is a strength in declarative statements, as different types of observation may be understood using the sentence's structure, which allows for comparisons between studies and the development of a knowledge based upon the research's findings. If a range facet is included in a declarative mapping sentence, then this range will tend to be stated in broad terms. It should be noted that in the examples of declarative mapping sentences I provided earlier in this chapter, the one example with a range facet, the mapping sentence taken from Wihlborg et al. (2019), is not a true response range, as respondents did not provide their answers to questions along this range. Rather, the mapping sentence took the form of a declarative mapping sentence which was used to define and develop qualitative research. Only after this research had been undertaken did the researchers perform a secondary analysis of the qualitative information that arose from group discussions and allocate these to one of the dichotomous options on what they called an "organisation range", which they used to organise the qualitative content of their mapping sentence. In this example, when taken together with its ontological and mereological characteristics, the organisational range will denote the epistemological characteristics of the observations that constitute the mapping sentence's logic, rather than limiting the way in which subjects are permitted to respond.

The preceding examples demonstrate that the best way to think of a declarative mapping sentence is as a set of categorial facets that have specified sub-components which form a definition of a bounded conceptual or research domain. The possible ways in which facets, facet elements, and indeed the whole mapping sentence are leant trustworthiness is through the range facet in the traditional mapping sentence, whereas, in both the traditional and declarative mapping sentence, the logical and cogent relationships between the specified structure of facet elements and real-world events and other theoretical constructs and considerations establish the sentence's veracity. A declarative mapping sentence will tend to facilitate understanding of a wider conceptual domain than the traditional mapping sentence. For example, if using a declarative mapping sentence, the researcher could ask participants to critically think about a specific place. In this situation, the declarative mapping sentence would offer a framework the researcher could use to interpret interviews and observational and other forms of qualitative data, which could be integrated in reference to how such information relates to different combinations of the facets and facet elements.

The Declarative Mapping Sentence as a Structured Mereology and Structured Ontology

The claims that I made earlier are broad, and during the remainder of this book, I will attempt to provide further support and justification for these. Earlier, I noted that when adopting a philosophical facet theory orientation, any form of mapping sentence may be thought of as a categorial ontology with the ability to establish and uphold hermeneutic consistency in research findings. Mapping sentences possess this ability because of the declarative mapping sentence being a structured ontology and structured mereology.

The phrase *hermeneutic consistency* can be found in the work of Martin Heidegger (2008) and Hans-Georg Gadamer (2004). In their formative writing, these authors were concerned with the interpretation of qualitative information and how such understandings are construed along with how these interpretations are associated with notions of truth and knowledge. On such understandings, hermeneutic consistency is associated with the ability of a researcher to establish explanations that are reliable, where *reliability* means the ability of a research instrument to yield consistent results when administered several times under similar circumstances. Reliability is achieved through the declarative mapping sentence's ontological and mereological components when these components accurately represent the domain of interest. When a mapping sentence does indeed embody hermeneutic consistency, it has the potential to elucidate understanding through the structure of its mapping sentence components, which may be adapted to address specific situations. Thus, in the case of the declarative mapping sentence, hermeneutic consistency is afforded through consideration of ontological and mereological aspects of the domain of interest. With this in mind, I will now provide further details regarding the meaning of these two terms.

Ontology and Mereology

As Lawson (2014) notes, *ontology* comes from the Greek word "onto", which has the meaning of "being", coupled with the Greek word "logos", which is taken to be "science". Thus, the study or science of being is contained within the word *ontology*, and this is how it is usually understood. However, this definition raises the question of what we understand by the word *being*. Lawson (2014) defines *being* in two ways, as some thing or entity that exists and also as what it is to actually be or exist. Consequently, he states, that for ontology to be the investigation of being, it must at the minimum include an examination of what exists, what is, and the nature of particular things that exist and how these things exist. Areas in which the term *ontology* are used include the disciplines of technology, logic, and computer sciences. Here, ontology can be understood as respectively meaning a systematic explanation of existence, a set of entities that are presumed extant priori to a theory, information and the diligent stating of the components that exist (sorts and characteristics), and the typical ways these interact. In the present writing, all of the preceding understandings of ontology are used to inform my specific view which emphasises understanding the nature of being (Poli and Seibt, 2014).

It is possible, when considering the definitions of ontology provided in technology, logic, and computer sciences to discern a commonality that runs through these. This thread is that all emphasise ideas about characteristics of being and existence in a primary, necessary, or fundamental sense that exists prior to deliberations about the substantive area of concern. When we are attempting to understand some form of complex behaviour, experience, state of affairs, and so on, it is likely that we may claim that this area of interest is composed of parts and that understanding the parts and their composition aids understanding of the phenomenon. This notion is supported by research into modularity, which focusses upon characteristics such as cognition and cognitive abilities. Here, it is widely understood that these entities are made up of components that may be separately identified but which may operate either separately or within a broad diversity of combinations.

In an attempt to remove any confusion due to the multiple understandings of the word *ontology*, a specific understanding of the word is used in this book. I define ontology in the following way:

- An ontology is a set of categories or concepts of a specific subject domain or area that are stated formally and explicitly.
- These categories are rudimentary or fundamental to the domain of interest.
- Ontology is concerned with the properties of the components of the ontology and the relationships within the ontology.

From a philosophical perspective, a declarative mapping sentence is an ontology that has the specific objective of defining a substantive research or conceptual research domain or area of understanding. The researcher attempts to identify and include within a declarative mapping sentence the fundamental aspects of an area of interest. The examples I have provided in this chapter of the use of the declarative mapping sentence, in areas such as the evaluation of IT systems (Zhang et al., 2016), the process of sacralisation (Przybylska, 2014), and the perception of three-dimensional abstract art (Hackett, 2017c) have all identified the rudimentary aspects of their relative domains and included these within declarative mapping sentences. My purpose in defining my use of the term *ontology* is to facilitate my defence of the use of this term in relation to personal and social behaviours and experiences, which are the main areas to which the declarative mapping sentence is applied.

As well as being ontologies, declarative mapping sentences are structured ontologies. The phrase *structured ontology* brings together ideas regarding the rudimentary aspects of being or experience (ontology) in relation to an area of interest along with conceptions regarding the way in which an ontology is organised or arranged (structure). On such an understanding, a declarative mapping sentence is a structured ontology that has been formally stated in an attempt to explain and understand an area of interest. The word *structured* in the phrase *structured ontology* lays emphasis upon notions of the ontology being arranged in a systematised way or determinately arranged and that by forming a systematised arrangement of the fundamental aspects of a research area, knowledge and understanding about this domain will be explicated. The researcher essentially uses the facets and facet elements of a declarative mapping sentence as a framework within which to develop and extend understanding of the domain of interest. This development comes about as the declarative mapping sentence provides a scaffold around which ontological components may vary in terms of the arrangement of their facet and element composition. Indeed, the declarative mapping sentences that I have provided as examples from the research of Zhang et al. (2016), Przybylska (2014), and Hackett (2017c) are structured ontologies where the declarative mapping sentences for each of the studies had a unique structure that reflected the subject's experience of his or her ontological content domain.

When investigating an area of interest, such as behaviours, experiences, and so on, not only will such a domain possess fundamental categories or components, but the domain will have characteristic and specific part-to-whole and part-to-part relationships. Mereology is concerned with theories of such part-to-whole relationships and has been defined as: "any theory of part hood or composition" (Harte, 2002, p. 7). The word *mereology* comes from the Greek word *meros*, which means "parts," and mereology addresses the logic of parts and wholes and any form of parthood relations. Examples of parthood include parts of the month such as weeks; "parts of a number series (e.g., the natural numbers) or, more directly of interest to the metaphysician, parts of things like structural universals" (Effingham, 2013, p. 152).

Mereology is most often applied to the understanding of the composition of material objects of some form (Effingham, 2013), and when we think of a material object, such as a car, we have little problem conceiving of the car as possessing parts, for example, an engine, wheels, lights, and so on, However, states of affairs also come under the purview of mereological consideration, and again, there is little difficulty thinking of states of affairs as possessing parts. The breadth of mereology's applicableness is demonstrated in Gorgio Lando's work when he states that mereological study can consider "parts and wholes in living organisms, social entities, in mathematics, and so on" (Lando, 2017, p. 3). According to Katherine Hawley (2017), metaphysical mereology is an area that has seen a resurgence after having become less popular since its peak some 50 years ago. She proposes that we now have the "resources to rehabilitate the mereological view of social groups" (Hawley, 2017, p. 395). Hawley goes on to emphasise that committees are social groups with members as their parts and are appropriate subject matter for a theory of parthood. Many other social groups, such as recreational reading groups, rock bands, and so on are, she claims, also social groups which are singular, concrete, composite particulars with parts that include human beings.[11] However, the attributes such as opinions, standards, customs, and so on that underlie associations between individual people and groups may be very different. Lando (2017) highlights the controversy when considering social entities and institutions as mereologies. He provides the example of parliament as being a social entity and institution. He then asks the question as to whether parliament can be thought of as having parts at all or whether notions of parts are being simply employed metaphorically to denote a social relation of the right to enter the house and participate in decision making. David-Hillel Ruben made several objections to a mereological view of social groups, expressing his belief that the relationships that people had to social groups did not have the relation of forming a part of the social entity (Ruben, 1983). A deeper consideration of mereology is beyond the scope of the present book, but on the understanding of mereology that I present in the following, when a declarative mapping sentence is developed, it is a statement of a content domain or area. Furthermore, this statement constitutes a structured ontology that embodies cognizance of the mereological relationships between ontological components within the domain of concern.

Mereology is an extremely uncommon term and is rarely, if ever, used outside of academia. However, within academia, mereology is employed differentially in the *sciences* (Calosi and Graziani, 2014), in *logic and mathematics* (Urbanaik, 2013), and in *semantics* (Moltmann, 2003). From within the discipline of philosophy (Henry, 1991), and especially metaphysics, mereology has the meaning of a theoretical understanding of parthood, the ways in which parts of a whole are related to the whole's other parts and to the composition of wholes. Because of this ambiguity in the usage of the term *mereology*, I offer a specific definition for the term as I have understood and employed this in the development and use of the declarative mapping sentence:

- Mereology is concerned with parthood through the unambiguous and methodical study and understanding of inter-relationships within ontologies of explicit structure.
- Such endeavour takes into account relationships of part to part, part to whole, part to context and background, and part to manifestations of understanding associated with the specified ontology.
- Context and background are indispensable and inherent components of the structured ontology's systemic realisation such that background and contextual alterations bring about significant differences in the systemic qualities of the structured ontology.
- Alteration in the manifestation of observation of the ontology would result in significant changes to the structured mereology or the meaning encompassed in the mereology.

The subject of this chapter, the declarative mapping sentence, on the preceding definition of mereology, clearly constitutes a mereology. This claim may be made as a declarative mapping sentence constitutes a compositional identity in the form of a proposition in regard to a specific area of interest. The declarative mapping sentence, when viewed both as a whole and in terms of the interrelationships present between its facets and facet elements, forms a mereological configuration. When a researcher is designing a declarative mapping sentence, he or she is so doing with the express intention of forming a representation of the content of interest whilst at the same time declaring what are believed to be the pertinent aspects of and inter-relationships within the domain. This declaration is in the form of facets and facet elements, connected in a way so as to reflect the real-life existence of the parts within the whole of the domain. As I have stated elsewhere (e.g., Hackett, 2018), the facets and their elements constitute the whole of the declarative mapping sentence in such a way that the whole is nothing more than its facet elemental components. To put this another way, the entirety of a declarative mapping sentence is its parts (facets and facet elements) (Cotnoir and Baxter, 2014).

It should be noted that the connective elements of a mapping sentence (the words and phrases that are used to link facets together in a meaningful manner)[12] are pertinent parts of the mapping sentence. Indeed, these units are best thought of as being facets in their own right or facets of connectivity. It is important to address these connective parts of the sentence, which act as functors (Corver and Riemsdijk, 2001), as they largely determine the meaning contained in the sentence. Even if the functors in a declarative mapping sentence do not play such a large role in determining the meaning of a particular sentence, as the content facets, they at least contextualise the meaning of facets and facet elements within the research domain. When taken together, the functors, facets, and facet elements in a declarative mapping sentence

- explicitly define a specific content domain
- form a template to enable the study of this domain in terms of the fundamental properties of the research area
- permit the research domain to be broken down in a systematic way that allows consideration of how sub-aspects of the domain interact
- facilitate greater understanding of the whole and an integrated understanding of the domain
- offer a framework within which to transmit the findings of the research which facilitates the development of a comparable and cumulative body of knowledge
- offer an interpretation of a specific content of interest that embodies consistent meaning and structure across studies that employ the declarative mapping sentence in their designs

By stating the content under enquiry, the declarative mapping sentence is able to play a role of cardinal importance to qualitative research by

- specifying the respondents along with the type of information that the researcher is gathering in order to investigate the mapping sentence's structure, thus permitting the testing of the hypothesised structure of the facets and facet elements proposed in the declarative mapping sentence
- facilitating theory development related to the pertinent features associated with the complexity present in research into specific behaviours, states of affairs, and so on

The declarative mapping sentence, when considered as a whole, is able to possess the preceding characteristics through using linguistic categories in order to place boundaries around a research area. A similar boundary placing function is also enacted upon the facets or important aspects of a specified research domain which are unequivocally stated as the terms of enquiry in reference to the domain. Through conspicuously sub-dividing facets into mutually exclusive sub-categories or conditions (elements), the variables or aspects that are believed to be important to a research domain are further signified.

The declarative mapping sentence is therefore a theoretical proposition, a declaration of a mapping of content facets into a research domain in the adaptable shape of a template for designing, analysing, and understanding research. When first stated, a declarative mapping sentence constitutes a set of possible theories about how the ways in which the elements within the sentences' specified facets may combine to allow a contextualised description of the specified domain. On this understanding, a declarative mapping is not a static end point in a piece of research, but rather it is an active and ongoing process that systematically suggests further possibilities regarding how to understand the domain of interest. When a facet element is selected from each of the facets and combined into a specific instance of a declarative mapping, the sentence is a definitional statement which assumes the role of a propositional sentence that puts forth the combinatorial logic of a facet element description of a specific instantiation of the content domain. After formulating a declarative mapping sentence, a researcher will then design instruments or enquiries and collect qualitative data or analyse the domain from within a facet-theoretical philosophical perspective so as to interrogate the hypothesised structure in the declarative mapping sentence.

Notes

1. In Hackett (2020), I present an example of the use of both traditional and declarative mapping sentences to view and explore a single content area, which in this example is bird behaviour.
2. See Polit and Beck (2010) for a discussion on generalising from qualitative and quantitative data.

3. It should be noted that some researchers would not recognise the lack of comparability as a problem but as a central strength in their work. This is a perspective with which I have considerable sympathy. However, I believe that there are many instances where comparability between qualitative research studies would constitute a considerable advantage. I comment further on this later in this chapter.
4. Whilst it is the case that the declarative mapping sentence has been developed primarily for use within qualitative forms of scholarship, the approach may also be used as a tool for clarifying and defining research concepts that will be quantitatively investigated.
5. An alternate perspective to the aesthetic orientation is provided by the institutional definition of art, and interested readers are guided to Dickie (1974, 2000), Bachrach (1977), Fokt (2013), Oppy (1991), Stecker (1986), and Wollheim (1987) for a discussion of this.
6. Crowther's model is made up of features such as style, image, temporality, metaphysical depth, notions of the art canon, context, and cognitive structure. I discuss these later in this chapter.
7. It has been noted that precision in concept development is of extreme importance (Klein and Delery, 2012; Locke, 2012; Osigweh, 1989; Skilton, 2011; Yaniv, 2011).
8. This may include alluding to synonyms, antonyms, analogies, and metaphors.
9. The authors noted that the two-facet example was a simplified rendition for illustrative purposes and acknowledged that other facets could have been included, such as "evaluative stakeholder with elements of user, senior manager, developer, vendor, consultant, and so on)" (Zhang et al., 2016, p. 6).
10. Within the facet theory literature, element profiles are known as structuples.
11. This is a mereological perspective of social groups. Such a view was in favour a few decades ago. However subsequent to criticisms by David-Hillel Ruben, notions of social mereology became unpopular.
12. Within a declarative mapping sentence, language is used so as to insinuate the roles that facets and their elements play in respect to the domain of research interest.

References

American Psychological Association. (2020a) *Positivism*, APA Dictionary of Psychology: Constructivism. Retrieved from https://dictionary.apa.org/constructivism.

American Psychological Association. (2020b) *Constructivism*, APA Dictionary of Psychology: Positivism. Retrieved from https://dictionary.apa.org/positivism.

Bachrach, J.E. (1977) Dickie's Institutional Definition of Art: Further Criticism, *The Journal of Aesthetic Education*, 11(3) pp. 25–35.

Bilska-Wodecka E., (2012) *Człowiek religijny i związki wyznaniowe w przestrzeni miasta w XX i na początku XXI wieku*, Instytut Geografii i Gospodarki Przestrzennej UJ, Kraków.

Calosi, C. and Graziani, P. (eds.) (2014) *Mereology and the Sciences: Parts and Wholes in the Contemporary Scientific Context*, New York: Springer.

Cooke, P.C., and Tredennick, T. (1938) *Aristotle: Categories. On Interpretation. Prior Analytics* (Loeb Classical Library No. 325), Cambridge, MA: Harvard University Press.

Corver, N., and Riemsdijk, H. (2001) Semi-lexical Categories, in Riemsdijk, H., van der Hulst, H., and Koster, J. (eds.) Semi-lexical Categories: The Function of

Content Words and the Content of Function Words, New York and Berlin: Mouton de Gruyer, 1–20.

Cotnoir, A.J., and Baxter, D.L.M. (eds.) (2014) *Composition as Identity*, Oxford: Oxford University Press.

Crowther, P. (2007) Defining Art, Creating the Canon: Artistic Value in an Era of Doubt, Oxford: Oxford University Press.

Davie G. (2013) *Sociology of religion. A critical agenda*, Sage publications, London.

Dickie, G. (1974) *Art and the Aesthetic: An Institutional Analysis*, Ithaca, NY: Cornell University Press.

Dickie, G. (2000) The Institutional Theory of Art, in Carrol, N. (ed.) *Theories of Art Today*, Madison: University of Wisconsin Press. pp 93–108.

Doll, W.J., and Torkzadeh, G. (1988) The Measurement of End-User Computing Satisfaction, *MIS Quarterly*, 12(2), 259–274.

Durning, S.J., Dong, T., Artino, A.R., van der Vleuten, C., Holmboe, E., and Schuwirth, L. (2015) Dual Processing Theory and Experts' Reasoning: Exploring Thinking on National Multiple-choice Questions, *Perspectives on Medical Education*, 4, 168–175.

Edwards, I., Jones, M., Carr, J., Braunack-Mayer, A., and Jensen, G.M. (2004) Clinical Reasoning Strategies in Physical Therapy, *Physical Therapy*, 84(4), 312–330. https://doi-org.ezp.lib.cam.ac.uk/10.1093/ptj/84.4.312

Effingham, N. (2013) *An introduction to ontologies*. Malden, MA: Polity Press.

Ekman, I., Swedberg, K., Taft, C., Lindseth, A., Norberg, A., Brink, E., Carlsson, J., Dahlin-Ivanoff, S., Johansson, I.L., Kjellgren, K., Liden, E., Ohlen, J., Olsson, L.E., Rosen, H., Rydmark, M., and Sunnerhagen, K.S. (2011) Person-centered Care – Ready for Prime Time, *European Society of Cardiology*, 10, 248–251.

Eva, K.W. (2005) What every teacher needs to know about clinical reasoning. Med. Educ. 39, 98–106.

Fokt, S. (2013) Solving Wollheim's Dilemma: A Fix for the Institutional Definition of Art, *Metaphilosophy*, 44(5), pp 640–654.

Gadamer, H.G. (2004) *Truth and Method (Wahrheit und Methode)*, New York: Crossroad.

Geertz, C. (1973) *The interpretation of cultures: Selected essays*. New York, NY: Basic Books.

Gorli, M., Kaneklin, C., & Scaratti, G. (2012) A multi-method approach for looking inside healthcare practices. Qualitative Research in Organizations and Management, 7(3), 290–307. doi:http://dx.doi.org.ezp.lib.cam.ac.uk/10.1108/174656412 11279761

Greggor, A.L., and Hackett, P.M.W. (2018) Categorization by the Animal Mind, in Hackett, P.M.W. (ed.) *Mereologies, Ontologies and Facets: The Categorial Structure of Reality*, Lanham, MD: Lexington Publishers.

Gruber, T.R. (1993) A Translation Approach to Portable Ontology Specifications, *Knowledge Acquisition*, 5(2), 199–220.

Guttman, L. (1954a) An Outline of Some New Methodology for Social Research, *Public Opinion Quarterly*, 18(4), 395–404.

Guttman, L. (1954b) A New Approach to Factor Analysis: The Radex, in P.F. Lazarsfeld (ed.) *Mathematical Thinking in the Social Sciences*, New York: Free Press, 258–348.

Guttman, L. (1971) Measurement as Structural Theory, *Psychometrika*, 36(4), 329–347.

Guttman, R., and Greenbaum, C.W. (1998) Facet Theory: Its Development and Current Status, *European Psychologist*, 3(1), 13–36.

Hackett, P.M.W. (1983) *Observations on Blink Rates in Ferruginous Duck (Aythya Nyroca) in a Flock of Mainly Mallard (Anas Platyrhynchos)*, Working Paper/Field Notes.

Hackett, P.M.W. (2013) *Fine Art and Perceptual Neuroscience: Field of Vision and the Painted Grid, Explorations in Cognitive Psychology Series*, London: Psychology Press.

Hackett, P.M.W. (2014a) *Facet Theory and the Mapping Sentence: Evolving Philosophy, Use and Application*, Basingstoke: Palgrave.

Hackett, P.M.W. (2014b) A Facet Theory Model for Integrating Contextual and Personal Experiences of International Students, *Journal of International Students*, 4(2), 164–176.

Hackett, P.M.W. (2015) Classifying Reality, by David S. Oderberg (ed.) (2013) Chichester: Wiley-Blackwell, *Frontiers in Psychology, Section Theoretical and Philosophical Psychology*, 6, 461. https://doi.org/10.3389/fpsyg.2015.00461.

Hackett, P.M.W. (2016a) *Psychology and Philosophy of Abstract Art: Neuroaesthetics, Perception and Compensation*, Basingstoke: Palgrave McMillan Publishers.

Hackett, P.M.W. (2016b) Facet Theory and the Mapping Sentence as Hermeneutically Consistent Structured Meta-Ontology and Structured Meta-Mereology, *Frontiers in Psychology, Section Theoretical and Philosophical Psychology*, 7, 471. https://doi.org/10.3389/fpsyg.2016.00471.

Hackett, P.M.W. (2017a) Commentary: Wild Psychometrics: Evidence for 'General' Cognitive Performance in Wild New Zealand Robins, Petroica Longipes, *Frontiers in Psychology, Section Theoretical and Philosophical Psychology*, 8, 165. https://doi.org/10.3389/fpsyg.2017.00165.

Hackett, P.M.W. (2017b) Editorial: Conceptual Categories and the Structure of Reality: Theoretical and Empirical Approaches, *Frontiers in Psychology, Section Theoretical and Philosophical Psychology*, 8, 601. https://doi.org/10.3389/fpsyg.2017.00601.

Hackett, P.M.W. (2017c) Opinion: A Mapping Sentence for Understanding the Genre of Abstract Art Using Philosophical/Qualitative Facet Theory, *Frontiers in Psychology, section Theoretical and Philosophical Psychology*, October 2017, 8, DOI: 10.3389/fpsyg.2017.01731.

Hackett, P.M.W. (2018a) Declarative Mapping Sentence Mereologies: Categories from Aristotle to Lowe, in Hackett, P.M.W. (ed.) *Mereologies, Ontologies and Facets: The Categorial Structure of Reality*, Lanham, MD: Lexington Publishers.

Hackett, P.M.W. (2018b) Introduction. Theoretical and Applied Categories in Philosophy and Psychology, in Hackett, P.M.W. (ed.) *Mereologies, Ontologies and Facets: The Categorial Structure of Reality*, Lanham, MD: Lexington Publishers.

Hackett, P.M.W. (2019a) Facet Mapping Therapy: The Potential of a Facet Theoretical Philosophy and Declarative Mapping Sentences Within a Therapeutic Setting, *Frontiers in Psychology, Section Psychology for Clinical Settings*. https://doi.org/10.3389/fpsyg.2019.0122.

Hackett, P.M.W. (2019b) Declarative Mapping Sentences as a Co-ordinating Framework for Qualitative Health and Wellbeing Research, *Journal of Social Science & Allied Health Professions*, 2(1), E1–E6.

Hackett, P.M.W. (2020) *The Complexity of Bird Behaviour: A Facet Theory Approach*, Cham, CH: Springer.

Hackett, P.M.W., Lou, L., and Capobianco, P. (2018) Integrating and Writing-up Data Driven Quantitative Research: From Design to Result Presentation, in Hackett, P.M.W. (ed.) *Quantitative Research Methods in Consumer Psychology: Contemporary and Data Driven Approaches*, London: Routledge.

Hackett, P.M.W., Schwarzenbach, J.B., and Jurgens, A.M. (2016) *Consumer Psychology: A Study Guide to Qualitative Research Methods*, Leverkusen: Barbara Budrich Publishers.

Hackett, P.M.W., Sepúlveda, J., and McCarthy, K. (2011) Improving Climate Change Education: A Geoscientific and Psychological Collaboration, in Fisher, Y., and Hans, S.L., Bernstein, V.J., and Marcus, J. (1985) Some Uses of the Facet Approach in Child Development, in Canter, D. (ed.) *Facet Theory: Approaches to Social Research*, New York: Springer Verlag, 151–172.

Harte, V. (2002) *Plato on Parts and Wholes: The Metaphysics of Structure*, Oxford: Oxford University Press.

Havlíček T., Hupková M., (2013) *Sacred structures in the landscape: The case of rural Czechia*, Scottish Geographical Journal 129(2), 100–121. doi:10.1080/14702541.2012.754931

Hawley, K. (2017) Social Mereology, *Journal of the American Philosophical Association*, 3(4), 395–411. https://doi.org/10.1017/apa.2017.3.

Heidegger, M. (2008) *Being and Time*, New York: Harper Perennial Modern Classics.

Henderson, V. (1991) *The Nature of Nursing: A Definition and Its Implications for Practice, Research, and Education: Reflections After 25 Years*, New York: National League for Nursing Press.

Henry, D.P. (1991) *Medieval Mereology*, Amsterdam: B.R. Grüner Publishing Company.

Ives, B., Olson, M.H., and Baroudi, J.J. (1983) The Measurement of User Information Satisfaction, *Communications of the ACM*, 26(10), 785–793.

Kaplan, M.A. (1964) *The Conduct of Inquiry: Methodology for Behavioral Science*, San Francisco, CA: Chandler Publishing Co.

Kim, S., Phillips, W.R., Pinsky, L., Brock, D., Phillips, K., and Keary, J. (2006) A Conceptual Framework for Developing Teaching Cases: A Review and Synthesis of the Literature Across Disciplines, *Medical Education*, 40, 867–876.

Klein, H.J., and Delery, J.E. (2012) Construct Clarity in Human Resource Management Research: Introduction to the Special Issue, *Human Resource Management Review*, 22(2, SI), 57–61.

Klima E. (2011) *Przestrzeń religijna miasta*, Wydawnictwo Uniwersytetu Łódzkiego, Łódź.

Koval, E.M., Hackett, P.M.W., and Schwarzenbach, J.B. (2016) Understanding the Lives of International Students: A Mapping Sentence Mereology, in Bista, K., and Foster, C. (eds.) *International Student Mobility, Services, and Policy in Higher Education*, Hershey, PA: IGI Global Publishers.

Lando, G. (2017) *Mereology: A Philosophical Introduction*, London: Bloomsbury.

Lange, D. (2008) A Multidimensional Conceptualization of Organizational Corruption Control, *Academy of Management Review*, 33(3), 710–729.

Lawson, T. (2014) A Conception of Social Ontology, in Pratten, S. (ed.) *Social Ontology and Modern Economics*, London: Routledge, 19–52.

Levett-Jones, T., Hoffman, K., Dempsey, J., Jeong, S.Y., Noble, D., Norton, C.A., Roche, J., and Hickey, N. (2010) The 'Five Rights' of Clinical Reasoning: An Educational Model to Enhance Nursing Students' Ability to Identify and Manage Clinically 'At Risk' Patients, *Nurse Education Today*, 30, 515–520.

Levy, S. (1990) The mapping sentence in cumulative theory construction: Wellbeing as an example', in Hox, J.J., and deJong-Gierveld, J. (eds.), *Operationalization and Research Strategy*, Amsterdam: Swets and Zeitlinger, pp. 155–177.

Lincoln, Y., and Guba, E. (1985) Naturalistic Inquiry, Beverly Hills, CA: Sage.

Locke, E.A. (2012) Construct Validity vs. Concept Validity, *Human Resource Management Review*, 22(2), 146–148.

Lou, L., and Hackett, P.M.W. (2018) *Qualitative Facet Theory and the Declarative Mapping Sentence, Contemporary Data Interpretations: Empirical Contributions in the Organizational Context*. Paper Presented at Organization 4.1: The role of values in Organizations of the 21st Century.

MacKenzie, S.B., Podsakoff, P.M., and Podsakoff, N.P. (2011) Construct Measurement and Validation Procedures in MIS and Behavioral Research: Integrating New and Existing Techniques, *MIS Quarterly*, 35(2), 293–334.

Marcum, J.A. (2012) An Integrated Model of Clinical Reasoning: Dual-process Theory of Cognition and Metacognition, *Journal of Evaluation in Clinical Practice*, 18, 954–961.

Mauffette-Leenders, L.A., Erskine, J.A., and Leenders, M.R. (2005) *Learning with Cases* (3rd ed.), London, Ontario: Richard Ivey School of Business.

McGrath, J.E. (1968) A Multi-Facet Approach to Classification of Individual Group and Organizational Concepts, in *People, Groups, and Organizations*, New York: Teachers College Press, 191–215.

McGrath, J.E. (1984) *Groups: Interaction and Performance*, Englewood Cliffs, NJ: Prentice-Hall.

Moltmann, F. (2003) *Parts and Wholes in Semantics*, Oxford: Oxford University Press.

Oppy, G. (1991) On Davies Institutional Definition of Art, *The Southern journal of philosophy*, 29(3), pp. 371–382.

Osigweh Yg, C.A.B. (1989) Concept Fallibility in Organizational Science, *Academy of Management Review*, 14(4), 579–594.

Petter, S., Straub, D., and Rai, A. (2007) Specifying Formative Constructs in Information Systems Research, *MIS Quarterly*, 31(4), 623–656.

Poli, R., and Seibt, J. (2014) *Theory and Applications of Ontology: Philosophical Perspectives*, New York: Springer.

Polit, D.F., and Beck, C.T. (2010) Generalization in Quantitative and Qualitative Research: Myths and Strategies, International Journal of Nursing Studies, 47(11), 1451–1458. https://doi.org/10.1016/j.ijnurstu.2010.06.004

Przybylska, L. (2014) *A Mapping Sentence for the Process of Sacralisation: The Case Study od Gdynia*, Prace Geograficzne, zeszyt 137, Kraków, PL: Instytut Geografii i Gospodarki Przestrzennej UJ, https://doi.org/10.4467/20833113PG.14.012.2157.

Ruben, D.-H. (1983) Social Wholes and Parts, Mind, 92, 219–238.

Schwab, D.P. (1980) Construct Validity in Organizational Behavior, *Research in Organizational Behavior*, 2, 3–43.

Schwarzenbach, J.B., & Hackett, P.M.W. (2015) *Transatlantic Reflections on the Practice-Based Ph.D. in Fine Art*, New York: Routledge Publishers.

Shkoler, O., Rabenu, E., Hackett, P.M.W., and Capobianco, P.M. (2020) *International Student Mobility and Access to Higher Education* (Marketing and Communication in Higher Education), Basingstoke: Palgrave MacMillan.

Shye, S., Elizur, D., and Hoffman, M. (1994) *Introduction to Facet Theory: Content Design and Intrinsic Data Analysis in Behavioral Research*, Thousand Oaks, CA: Sage Publications, Inc.

Skilton, P.F. (2011) Getting the Reader to 'I Get It!: Clarification, Differentiation and Illustration, *Journal of Supply Chain Management*, 47(2), 22–28.

Sołjan, I. (2012) *Sanktuaria i ich rola w organizacji przestrzeni miast na przykładzie największych europejskich ośrodków katolickich*, Instytut Geografii i Gospodarki Przestrzennej UJ, Kraków.

Stecker, R. (1986) The End of an Institutional Definition of Art, *British Journal of Aesthetics*, 26(2) p124–132. doi: 10.1093/bjaesthetics/26.2.124

Straub, D., Boudreau, M.-C., and Gefen, D. (2004) Validation Guidelines for IS Positivist Research, *Communications of the Association for Information Systems*, 13(1), 24.

Suddaby, R. (2010) Editor's Comments: Construct Clarity in Theories of Management and Organization, *Academy of Management Review*, 35(3), 346–357.

Theije de M. (2012) *Reading the city religious: Urban transformation and social reconstruction in Recife, Brasil*, [in:] R. Pixten, L. Dikomitis (eds.), *When God comes to town: Religious traditions in urban contexts*, Berghahn Books, New York, 97–113.

Townsend, A., Cox, S.M., and Li, L.C. (2010) Qualitative Research Ethics: Enhancing Evidence-Based Practice in Physical Therapy, *Physical Therapy*, 90(4). 615–628, https://doi-org.ezp.lib.cam.ac.uk/10.2522/ptj.20080388

Urbanaik, R. (2013) *Leśniewski's Systems of Logic and Foundations of Mathematics*, New York: Springer.

Van de Ven, A.H. (2007) Building a Theory, in Van de Ven, A.H. (ed.), *Engaged Scholarship a Guide for Organizational and Social Research*, Oxford: Oxford University Press.

Weber, R. (2012) Evaluating and Developing Theories in the Information Systems Discipline, *Journal of the Association for Information Systems*, 13(1), 1–30.

Wihlborg, J., Edgren, G., Johansson, A., and Sivberg, B. (2019) Christina Gummesson (2019) Using the Case Method to Explore Characteristics of the Clinical Reasoning Process Among Ambulance Nurse Students and Professionals, *Nurse Education in Practice*, 35, 48–54.

Wixom, B.H., and Todd, P.A. (2005) A Theoretical Integration of User Satisfaction and Technology Acceptance, *Information Systems Research*, 16(1), 85–102.

Wollheim, Richard. (1987) *Painting as Art*, Princeton: Princeton University Press.

Yaniv, E. (2011) Construct Clarity in Theories of Management and Organization, *Academy of Management Review*, 36(3), 590–592.

Zelinsky W. (2010) *Organizing religious landscapes*, [in:] M.P. Conzen (ed.), *The making of the American landscape*, Routledge, second edition, New York–London, 253–278.

Zhang, M., Gable, G., and Rai, A. (2016) Toward Principles of Construct Clarity: Exploring the Usefulness of Facet Theory in Guiding Conceptualization, *Australasian Journal of Information Systems*, 20. http://doi.org/10.3127/ajis.v20i0.1123.

4 Conclusion and Future Research

Content Summary

In this final chapter, I provide suggestions regarding the direction in which mapping sentence and declarative mapping sentence research may be taken. The suggestions that I make are based upon both my ongoing research in this area and that of others.

Introduction

In this final chapter, I reflect upon the declarative mapping sentence and qualitative uses of the facet theory perspective and further explore the theoretical underpinnings of these. I commence my examination by deliberating upon the similarities and differences between declarative and traditional forms of the mapping sentence. When talking about the declarative mapping sentence, Anna Marmodoro (2014) and Paul Capobianco (2018) describe some of the characteristics of this linguistic structure. Marmodoro emphasises the mereological nature of a declarative mapping sentence when she states that this linguistic structure is "something like the hypothesis of the existence of a certain specific combinatorial pattern in the way we [each individual] experience a certain sector of reality" (Marmodoro, 2014).

Paul Capobianco lays emphasis similarly upon the mereological structure of the declarative mapping sentence but stresses the invisibility of the sentence when it is being used to facilitate investigation into some behavioural or experiential segment:

> Facet theory and the mapping sentence is a philosophical disposition towards the understanding of behavioural complexities. It is a climbing frame that disappears when one reaches its summit.
>
> (Capobianco, 2018)

These two statements emphasise what I believe to be strengths of declarative mapping sentences: that these forms of sentences constitute hypothetical frameworks for exploring and understanding a research domain that do not get in the way, obscure, or distort the phenomenon that is under investigation.

The Semantic and Linguistic Structure of the Mapping Sentence

As well as containing a substantive content in regard to an area of research, all forms of mapping sentences also embody linguistic and semantic structures.[1] The linguistic components of a mapping sentence are the words and grammar which contain and transmit the sentence's meaning (the semantic sense). The linguistic validity of a mapping sentence is achieved through its ability to be used to design research that can directly draw upon and address the semantic sense of the sentence. All mapping sentences are developed in order to facilitate the asking of questions regarding specific complex behaviours, phenomena, states of affairs, and so on, where the questions are structured based upon an arrangement of aspects of the overall question in relation to the mapping sentence. A researcher's task is to evaluate these complex structures in terms of the extent to which the linguistic components in a mapping sentence characterise and correspond to the mapping sentence's semantic structure. Furthermore, the researcher must ensure that the parts of the proposed mapping sentence meaningfully interact within the proposed mapping sentence.

One of the major benefits a scholar may accrue when using either a declarative or traditional mapping sentence results from the time and effort that he or she must expend in determining the connective ontology employed in the mapping sentence. The importance of the connective words and phrases used in a mapping sentence is rooted in the intimacy of the connection between the linguistic and semantic aspects of the sentence. When using a mapping sentence, the researcher has to carefully select the pertinent variables and their sub-divisions for inclusion as facets and facet elements. They must also carefully and meaningfully inter-relate these variables using connective words and phrases, the selection of which is as important as the selection of facets and elements.

A declarative mapping sentence may have its usefulness tested and the truthful nature of its proposed contents examined through conducting research using the same declarative mapping sentence in order to design studies that are conducted at different times or in different places. If broadly similar results are obtained, or results that vary in explicable ways, the veracity and semantic coherence of the declarative sentence is upheld. In understanding the results that come out of the use of a declarative mapping sentence, it should be remembered that because of the multiple elements present in facets, the multipart structure of a mapping sentence is necessarily variable, and the elements' mutually exclusive nature may be related to the time and place of the use of the declarative mapping sentence. As different places or situations have different properties that may be meaningfully related to the content of the mapping sentence, a mapping sentence may have a different elemental structure in different times and places in which the mapping sentence is used. It is also important to note that the parts, or facets and elements, of a mapping sentence may be related to each other in different ways at different times and in different situations. A wide variety of aspects of any specific situation may influence both the facets and elements of a declarative mapping sentence and how these come together in a way that contains and transmits meaning.

Moltmann (1997, p. 2) illustrates how situations are complex and how time and place may impact upon our understanding of a research domain when he states that "Situations may include accidental properties of entities, and an entity may be an accidental integrated whole in one situation, but not in another". Moltmann's entity may be represented within a declarative mapping sentence, as such sentences are able to embody events. When designing a declarative mapping sentence, the researcher attempts to capture the totality of a phenomenon. However, as Moltmann says, a situation may incorporate incomplete evidence concerning an entity, and the characteristic of containing only some and not all possible information about an event is also analogous to what may be present in a declarative mapping sentence. In an attempt to take into account the influence of context upon a declarative mapping sentence, it is important that a declarative mapping sentence has components and a structure that

- combine so as to form an integrated and meaningful whole
- are variable in that the components and structure differ in different situations or when a different perspective is adopted when viewing the domain of the sentence

These requisites demonstrate that there is a negotiated and somewhat fluid relationship between the categorial structure of the declarative mapping sentence and the event, state of affairs, and so on that it is representing.

Further Understanding Mapping Sentences

The originator of facet theory and the traditional mapping sentence, Louis Guttman, stated, "A theory is an hypothesis of a correspondence between a definitional system for a universe of observations and an aspect of the empirical structure of those observations, together with a rationale for such an hypothesis" (in Borg, 1981, pp. 47–64; Gratch, 1973, p. 35; Guttman, 1982, pp. 331–348; Hackett, 2014; Levy, 1976, p. 117). On the understanding contained in Guttman's statement, a mapping sentence is a theory or a hypothesis in regard to the empirical nature of a domain under scrutiny. Guttman's words are apropos to the declarative mapping sentence as I have presented it, as declarative mapping sentences are essentially ways of proposing a theory for both the conception and development of research and scholarship as well as a theory about the fundamental aspects of the behaviour and experience that is the subject of the enquiry.

If we think about the ways that we use language in our daily lives, sentences are sophisticated parts of our language system, which we understand through the establishment of the meaning contained in single words[2] in tandem with the meaning that is present in the meaningful combination of verbs and their arguments.[3] We use words and sentences when we describe behaviour, even though simply attempting to define the term *word* in an unambiguous and non-contentious way is problematic (Lyons, 1977). This is due to the fact that the word *word* may refer to a lexeme[4] or to two different forms of a lexeme. Within a declarative mapping sentence, we use words as facet elements and as connective ontology between facets. In this context, for example, the words *experience*, *experiences*, and *experiencing* are different usages of the same word, where the context and precise subject of investigation that is being investigated determines the word that should be employed. Both declarative mapping sentences and everyday sentences permit the determining of the meanings of individual words within sentences in relation to the behavioural or experiential phenomenon of interest. Furthermore, both types of mapping sentences allow us to develop an understanding of a phenomenon by combining words within sentences (this is true in declarative mapping sentences and everyday sentences) when these are read as a whole sentence.

However, criticisms can be aimed at the declarative mapping sentence. One such reproach is that the declarative mapping sentence may be seen to provide a remedy to a problem that does not exist. What I mean by this is that for many, if not most, qualitative researchers, the great strength of this approach to research is the fact that the research is guided by the research participants rather than the researcher. This is especially true of a researcher working within a grounded theory perspective (see, for example, Bryant and Charmaz, 2007; Urquhart, 2012) or other similar approaches. In a grounded theory research study, the researcher adopts a systematic approach and methodology which employs an inductive rather than a deductive process in the development of theories to explain a body of data. Qualitative data are gathered in a methodological manner and may commence with a question. These data are then reviewed and re-reviewed, and recurring concepts and ideas emerge from this interrogation of the data. These regularities in the information collected in the research are noted and coded and brought together into conceptual groups and then into categories, and the categories may then be used to develop theoretical statements about the content domain being investigated.

The declarative mapping sentence may therefore appear to run counter to the grounded theory approach, and if the dicta of grounded theory are strictly applied, then this is indeed the case. In such circumstances, the use of a declarative mapping sentence would not be appropriate. Notwithstanding this, whilst my last statement is true, it is also the case that in many qualitative research studies, the researcher does not want to restrict his or her research to the investigation of pre-determined and a priori stated hypotheses. However, there are often times when a researcher wishes not to investigate the unspecified content implied in grounded theory. This is especially true of applied research that wishes to provide suggestions about specific phenomena but does not wish to be bound to asking specific pre-formulated questions. In this situation, the declarative mapping sentence is appropriate for designing research. I make this claim, as the declarative sentence specifies the area of interest in the form of facets and their interconnections based upon a literature search or some other preliminary enquiry. However, the precise questions or other activities associated with information gathering are left up to the researcher to determine and could indeed be left very unstructured.

Another point I must also mention is the position of the researcher. In quantitative or traditional scientific forms of enquiry, the role of the researcher is usually depicted as being neutral. In qualitative research, this is not the case, and probably most qualitative researchers would question the ability of a researcher to assume a neutral position in relation to either the research participants or the subject matter of the research. When using a declarative mapping sentence, the neutrality of the research may be treated as a facet of the enquiry with elements that express the extent to which the researcher was neutral or intimately implicated in the research process. In this way, the researcher's reflections upon the reflexive nature of his or her presence and the extent to which the information collected constituted the co-construction of the interviewee's responses are incorporated into the research process, interpretations, and findings.

Final Words

Traditionally, the mapping sentence, as I have described this, has been associated with quantitative research and data (for examples, see Canter, 1985b; Shye, 1978; Shye and Elizur, 1994; Borg and Shye, 1995). We have already considered how the traditional mapping sentence has been employed in a wide variety of theoretical and applied contexts. However, I have extended this research into qualitative arenas of enquiry, addressing such substantive fields as the perception of fine art (Hackett, 2016a, 2017) and avian behaviour, taxonomy, and so on (Hackett, 2020). Over the past few years, I have developed a qualitative or philosophical approach to facet theory, which has the *declarative mapping sentence* at its heart. My enquiries that led up to the origination of the declarative mapping sentence have used facet theory as a philosophical approach to research content (Hackett, 2013, 2014, 2016b). In the context of this book, the declarative mapping sentence, whilst growing out of qualitative scholarship, is also applicable as a tool for clarifying and defining quantitative research concepts.

As with all mapping sentences, the process of declarative mapping[5] is an all-inclusive representation of an area of research or content domain. The declarative mapping sentence achieves a comprehensive description of an area through stating as a sentence facets and elements with carefully selected connective phrases. The result is a sentence that meaningfully communicates the mereological interplay between the sentence's facets whilst linguistically suggesting the role of facets and elements in terms of the content domain. Thus, declarative mapping sentences are templates that convey the meaning of the domain and which transmit consistent meaning through their configurative qualities of parts in relation to the conceptual whole. The manner in which a declarative mapping sentence is different from other forms of mapping sentence is that the declarative mapping sentence typically does not have a range facet. In a further departure from the traditional mapping sentence, if a declarative mapping sentence does possess a range, the elements from the range may reference a broad conceptual area rather than applying to a specified question or instance. Thus, a declarative mapping sentence constitutes categorial facets with their respective elements that delimit (categorise) a research domain.

Mapping sentences possess a conceptual content linguistically specified in the facets and their elements along with words and phrases that connect these and which give the facet and elements meaning in relation to the content being described. On this understanding, a declarative mapping sentence allows the researcher to explicitly state and then study a research domain in terms of the fundamental or pertinent aspects of the research area, to systematically and thoroughly break down these major aspects of research content, and to evaluate the interplay of these sub-aspects in a way that may reveal meaning in terms of the research content as a whole. The declarative mapping sentence achieves the preceding by offering a meaningfully consistent framework for undertaking research.

Notes

1. Declarative mapping sentences are linguistic structures that represent a semantic entity on an understanding that linguistic units in themselves are categories (Taylor, 2003).
2. Within my writing about mapping sentences, words play a cardinal role. Obviously, words are also fundamental to the mapping sentence and understandings thereof. It is not within the scope of this short book to consider in any detail the conceptual basis of the words. For more details on words, see Taylor (Taylor, 2002, 2014, 2017).
3. The results from neurophysiological research into human subjects suggests we initially process word category information along with establishing local phrase structure. Later on in the processing process, other and different types of information are extracted. Even later, it appears that interaction between different types of information happens in what seems to be a universal order. The precise point at which these later forms of processing occur is dependent upon on when the relevant information becomes available (Friederici and Weissenborn, 2007).
4. Lexemes are a fundamental component of a language's lexicon. A lexeme possesses a meaning greater than that of its individual components (see glossary).
5. The process of declarative mapping results in a declarative mapping sentence, as a declarative mapping statement, or it may be formed as one of the mapping sentence types mentioned earlier in this chapter.

References

Borg, I. (ed) (1981) Multidimensional Data Representations: When & Why, Ann Arbor.

Borg, I., and Shye, S. (1995) *Facet Theory: Form and Content* (Advanced Quantitative Techniques in the Social Sciences), Thousand Oaks, CA: Sage Publications, Inc.

Bryant, A., and Charmaz, K. (eds.) (2007) *The SAGE Handbook of Grounded Theory*, Thousand Oaks, CA: Sage Publications.

Canter, D. (1985) How to Be a Facet Researcher, in Canter, D. (ed.) *Facet Theory: Approaches to Social Research*, New York: Springer Verlag, 265–276.

Gratch, H. (1973) Twenty-five Years of Social Research in Israel, Jerusalem Academic Press, Jerusalem.

Guttman, L. (1982) "What is not what" in theory construction. In Hauser, R.M., Mechanic, D. & Haller, A. (Ed.). *Social Structure and Behavior*. New York: Academic Press, 331–348.

Hackett, P.M.W. (2013) *Fine Art and Perceptual Neuroscience: Field of Vision and the Painted Grid*, New York: Psychology Press.

Hackett, P.M.W. (2014) *Facet Theory and the Mapping Sentence: Evolving Philosophy, Use and Application*, Basingstoke: Palgrave McMillan Publishers.

Hackett, P.M.W. (2016a) *Psychology and Philosophy of Abstract Art: Neuroaesthetics, Perception and Comprehension*, Basingstoke: Palgrave McMillan Publishers.

Hackett, P.M.W. (2016b) Facet Theory and the Mapping Sentence as Hermeneutically Consistent Structured Meta-Ontology and Structured Meta-Mereology, *Frontiers in Psychology, Section Theoretical and Philosophical Psychology.* https://doi.org/10.3389/fpsyg.2016.00471.

Hackett, P.M.W. (2017) *The Perceptual Structure of Three-Dimensional Art, Springer Briefs in Philosophy*, New York: Springer.

Hackett, P.M.W. (2020) *The Complexity of Bird Behaviour: A Facet Theory Approach*, Cham, CH: Springer.

Levy, S. (1976) Use of the mapping sentence for coordinating theory and research: a cross-cultural example. *Quality and Quantity: European-American Journal of Methodology*, 10: 117–125.

Lyons, J. (1977) *Linguistic Semantics, Volume 2*, Cambridge: Cambridge University Press.

Moltmann, F. (1997) *Parts and Wholes in Semantics*, Oxford: Oxford University Press.

Shye, S. (1978) *Theory Construction and Data Analysis in the Behavioral Sciences*, San Francisco, CA: Jossey-Bass.

Shye, S., and Elizur, D. (1994) *Introduction to Facet Theory: Content Design and Intrinsic Data Analysis in Behavioral Research* (Applied Social Research Methods), Thousand Oaks, CA: Sage.

Taylor, J.R. (2002) *Cognitive Grammar*, Oxford: Oxford University Press.

Taylor, J.R. (2003) *Linguistic Categorisation*, Oxford: Oxford University Press.

Taylor, J.R. (2014) *The Mental Corpus: How Language is Represented in the Mind*, Oxford: Oxford University Press.

Taylor, J.R. (ed.) (2017) *The Oxford Handbook of the Word*, Oxford: Oxford University Press.

Urquhart, C. (2012) *Grounded Theory for Qualitative Research: A Practical Guide*, Thousand Oaks, CA: Sage Publications.

Glossary

In this research, there are a series of terms that have been incorporated into the research that have specific or nuanced meaning. The following is a list of the precise meanings of these words and phrases along with further details of the terms and appropriate references.[1]

Category

A category is a class or some other form of partitioning or breaking up of things or people on the basis of these having some shared characteristic. In philosophy, categories are usually thought of as follows: "A system of categories is a complete list of highest kinds or genera" (Thomasson, 2018) or as an exhaustive set of classes within which everything may be allocated.

Clause

Traditionally, a clause is said to consist of a subject and predicate. It is a unit of grammatical organisation ordered directly below the sentence. It is the smallest unit in grammar that is able to express complete ideas. A clause may constitute a complete sentence in and of itself, or it may be part of a sentence. A main clause is a clause that is able to stand alone and forms a complete sentence, as it has a subject and predicate. A subordinate clause is dependent upon a main clause, is part of this main clause, and is usually preceded by a conjunction.

Cognition/Cognitive

Cognition and *cognitive* refer in some to way to the mental action of thinking and knowing. The American Psychological Association (2018) define cognition to include awareness and knowing – "perceiving, conceiving, remembering, reasoning, judging, imagining, and problem solving". Furthermore, the American Psychological Association state that traditionally the components of the mind are cognition, affect, and conation.

Concept

In philosophy, a *concept* is an important term in reason and language and is a mental representation or image, an idea that parallels an event or entity or class of events or entities or the indispensable aspects of the entity or event.

Connective Ontology

(See *ontology* [connective])

Construct

Within this book, I have used the term *construct* in a similar manner to the definition provided by the American Psychological Association (2018). Thus, I take a construct to be an exploratory theoretical model that is based upon empirical research or as a hypothetical model arrived at through inference from empirical data.

Declarative Mapping Sentence (DMS)

A declarative mapping sentence is a form of a traditional mapping sentence (see *mapping sentence* (in a general sense) later in this glossary). It has been developed by Paul Hackett (Hackett, 2014, 2016a-c, 2018) and is similar to its traditional counterpart except that it often does not include a range facet and is usually used in qualitative and philosophical research.

Element

(See *facet element*).

Facet (a)

A facet can be thought of as a variable, construct, or some other form of discretely identifiable component of a definition of a domain of research or important factor influencing a content that is under investigation. The facets that are specified for a research study, when taken together, constitute all of the variables that are of interest in the study. Facets are specified that are as much as is possible mutually exclusive in terms of their combined influence within the research area.

Facet Element

A facet element (or often just element) is a sub-division of a facet that is as near as possible mutually exclusive with other elements of a facet. Facet elements are not the means by which a mapping sentence is assessed, but they constitute the structure of the phenomenon under scrutiny. Elements should not be confused with a facet range (however, a range facet will also possess elements).

Facet Structure(s)

Facets possess a limited number of acceptable multi-dimensional structures that are pictured or represented in two-dimensional space.

Single-facet structures may take the following forms.

- Linear – in this situation, events are similar or dissimilar to each other, so they may be positioned on a straight line, and the similarities between event pairs are maintained (see Gabriel, 1954; Runkel and McGrath, 1972). This is called a *simplex*.
- Circular – in which a matrix of correlations between events is high along the diagonals and at each corner, and the correlations at the centre of the matrix are at their lowest (see Brown, 1985). This is called a *circumplex*.

Multiple-facet structures (also known as higher-order structures) come about when more than a single facet explains a content area and these facets interact. Examples of such multiple facet roles include the following:

- Two intersecting ordered facets (two simplex structures) form a *duplex* in which the two facets are positioned orthogonally to each other (see Elizur and Shye, 1976).
- A simplex intersects with a circumplex for a *radex* (Lingoes and Borg, 1977). Coxon (1982) states that this facet structure is depicted as a circumplex with multiple concentric circles that also has lines that originate at the centre of the circles and progress to the edge of the plot.

As well as two-facet structures, there are multi-facet structures that are made up of three facets, for example,

- The *cylindrex* is composed of two or more radex stacked one above the other (Brown, 1985). This structure comes about when a quantitative assessment (a simplex) combines with a qualitative evaluation (a circumplex) forming a radex, and the radex is independently associated with, or present at, a series of different levels of another ordered facet (see, for example, Hackett, 1995).

- The triplex is also a three-facet structure. However, this time, the three facets that combine are all ordered facets (simplexes) (for example, see Borg and Mohler, 2011).

The preceding higher-order structures (and other facet combinations that have not been presented) constitute complex spatial hypotheses that are the combinations to the more rudimentary hypotheses in the two-dimensional structures and are related to Guttman's work (Hildebrandt, 1986).

Facet Theory

Facet theory is a meta-theoretical approach to research design, implementation, and analysis (Canter, 1985; Hackett, 2014). Facet theory allows the mapping of some facet of an individual or group of people in reference to a process within a specified context. It achieves this through using a mapping sentence (facet theory's main research tool); the approach brings together a prescribed analysis of a research domain's contents with analytic approaches, such as smallest space analysis (SSA) and partial order scalogram analysis (POSA). These analyses are multidimensional. Facet theory integrates the design of research content with data analysis, which allows for meaningful appraisal of a research domain and permits the possibility of theory development (see Brown, 2010).

Guttman, Louis

Louis Guttman (1916–1987) was an American mathematician, sociologist, and professor of social and psychological assessment. He is best known for his scholarship in the area of social statistics and for his psychometric work (especially multidimensional scaling and his philosophical work on multidimensional analysis approaches), the origination of the Guttman Scale, and the development of facet theory.

Hermeneutical (Hermeneutics)

Hermeneutics is a branch of knowledge that is concerned with the content of narratives or texts. Specifically, hermeneutics is concerned with the interpretation of such texts, most commonly in the context of theological or literary texts.

Intelligence

There are different definitions of intelligence, but most involve notions of an individual's ability to develop and employ knowledge and skills.

Learning

Learning is demonstrated as a relatively permanent change in behaviour that is brought about through experience. Learning is a major component or type of avian cognition and is often assessed in research into the cognitive abilities of birds (for a contemporary example, see Lawrence and Noonan, 2018). Sub-types of learning in birds include social learning (e.g., Riebel et al., 2012) and song learning (Mennill et al., 2018; Rivera-Cáceres, 2017).

Mapping Sentence (in a General Sense)

A mapping sentence is a formal statement of the research project that is being conducted in the format of a natural language sentence (see Hackett, 2014, 2018). A mapping sentence has three types of facets (more on these later), each of which is linked to the others using connecting words to form a sentence with a structure that approximates normal prose. The sentence suggests the expected inter-relationship between the content facets within the context of the specified research inquiry. A mapping sentence is made up of three types or categories of information (these categories are called facets). The three types of facet are the background facet, the content facet, and the range facet. Background facets specify details of the events, people, or objects to be classified or investigated in the research project. Background facets may also be sub-divisions of the population under investigation that you believe to be important in understanding the content of the domain under enquiry. Content facets specify the research domain that will be investigated in the project. Content facets are the major sub-divisions of research content. For example, if your research project is investigating user experience of a certain place, the facets will be the major aspects of place experience that have been identified in prior research to be influential in effecting users when they are in that situation. The more complex the investigation is, the more content facets a project will contain. The range facet[2] specifies the overall orientation of the research project or is the measurement that will be taken in the research (for example, in assessing the user's experience of a place, the range facet may well be one of degree of satisfaction with the various aspects of place as specified in the content facet overall customer satisfaction).

Mapping Sentence Mereology

A mapping sentence is a sentence written in ordinary English prose which contains facets and elements and where the facets are the major components of a research domain and the elements are the exhaustive, mutually exclusive conditions of the facets. *Mapping sentence mereology* is a term used in qualitative or philosophical facet theory and with the declarative mapping sentence. Mapping sentence mereology refers to the inter-connections and inter-relationships between the facets and the facet elements in a mapping sentence (usually declarative) including the connective components and functors.

Mapping Sentence – Declarative

(See *declarative mapping sentence*).

Mapping Sentence – Traditional

(See *mapping sentence [in a general sense]*).

Mapping Sentence Ontology

A mapping sentence is a sentence written in ordinary English prose which contains facets and elements and where the facets are the major components of a research domain and the elements are the exhaustive, mutually exclusive conditions of the facets. *Mapping sentence ontology* is a term used in qualitative or philosophical facet theory and with the declarative mapping sentence. Mapping sentence ontology refers to the relationships and properties between the concepts and categories of a mapping sentence (usually declarative) including the connective components and functors.

Mereology

Mereology is the theoretical study of the relationship between parts in relation to the wholes they constitute and also of part to part within a whole (Varzi, 2016). It is a term typically found in philosophy and mathematical logic. The term *mereology* was originated by Leśniewski (1927–1931). Mereology has typically been used in reference to the parts of objects and metaphysics. However, mereology has also been employed in the investigation of social mereology (Hawley, 2017; Petranovich, 2018; Strohmaier, 2019). This has been somewhat controversial, and the legitimacy of considering people as parts of a committee in the same way that a nucleus is part of an atom and an engine is part of a car has been questioned (for example by Ruben [1983]).

Meta-Mereology

Meta-mereology has been used to mean "a thorough analysis of it" (mereology) (Pietruszczak, 2018). However, within this book, the term *meta-mereology* is used to mean a mereology of or about a mereology or mereology.

Meta-Ontology

I am using the term *meta-ontology* in the sense of it being a meta-theory of ontology. Consequently, a meta-ontology is an ontology of an ontology or a dialogue on an ontology and its methodological components.

New Zealand Robin

The New Zealand robin is a sexually dimorphic small dark-grey/black passerine with a light coloured front. The New Zealand robin has been split into two different species. These are the North Island robin (*Petroica longipes*) and the South Island robin (*Petroica australis*). However, the research reported in this book is concerned with the North Island robin (*Petroica longipes*). Previously, the two species were considered conspecific.

Ontology

Ontology is a term used in slightly different ways by several academic and work disciplines. Within this book, *ontology* will be understood as relationships and properties between a collection of concepts and categories within a specific domain of interest.

Oology

The word *oology* came from the Greek word "oion", which means egg. Oology is the study and collecting of birds' eggs along with the study of birds' nests and breeding behaviours. As a form of study, it is a branch of ornithology.

Partial Order Scalogram Analysis (POSA)

Partial order scalogram analysis (POSA) and its variant known as partial order scalogram analysis with base co-ordinates (POSAC) is a form of statistical analysis. I define *scalogram* in detail later in this glossary; however, at this point, it is important to note that a scalogram is a psychological assessment procedure in which for a respondent to respond correctly or to be able to accomplish a task at a given level means that he or she would have successfully completed all earlier items in the assessment. POSA analyses an individual respondent's profile of scalogram items. POSA produces a two-dimensional graphical plot of a multivariate data set which depicts each element as a point in this space. In these plots, points are located so the point that represents item A is positioned above the point representing item B if and only if A>B (see Raveh and Landau, 1993).

Phrase

In language, a phrase is a small collection of words that form a conceptual unit with an idiomatic meaning and which usually are part of a clause.

Predicate

We use the word *predicate* in its grammar sense. On this understanding, a predicate is a part of a sentence which contains a verb and which has reference to the sentence's subject.

Qualitative Research

Qualitative research is research that employs non-numerical assessment criteria and yields non-numerical data. This type of research typically produces text or observational or narrative data and cannot be analysed statistically. Qualitative research typically attempts to produce rich understanding of the research context with findings that cannot be applied with confidence outside of the sample being investigated.

Quantitative Research

Quantitative research produces numerical data that may be analysed statistically. This form of research may be generalised outside of the sample used in the research with a specific level of confidence regarding the robustness of such generalisations. Quantitative data and research are typically not used to reveal respondents' rich personal meanings.

Reliability

Reliability has a specific meaning in the context of research. On this meaning, reliability refers to the consistency and trustworthiness of a measure or assessment procedure. Therefore, what is meant by reliability is the extent to which a measure will produce the same result when it is applied on multiple occasions or at different times to the same sample.

Scalogram

The concept of the scalogram comes largely out of the work of Louis Guttman. A scalogram is a collection of questions or other means of gathering data about a given content area (see for example, Guttman, 1944). What is unique about the scalogram is that after considerable testing, a final set of questions or items is collected together and arranged in such a way that a positive response, accomplishing a given task at a given level, implies that all lower-level tests or items would also have been positively or successfully completed. The items themselves must focus upon a single area but may be drawn from many domains, such as being able to complete a mathematical test, being able to complete a puzzle, agreement with a series of propositions, and so on. A scalogram is a test of a cumulative ability or skill. An example would be a test of the cognitive ability of children. In this example, it would be expected that a child who could perform a mental multiplication would also be able to perform a written addition, and this child would also be able to identify a pile of a given number of items from another pile of a different number of items. In this example, a scalogram is formed where successfully performing the first task given predicts successful performance of the other tasks. This form of cumulative testing of ability has obvious benefit for use with birds that are not able to respond verbally to enquiries or report the process they go through to solve a problem.

Sentence

A sentence is a collection of words that may be thought of as being complete in themselves. Usually, a sentence contains a subject and a predicate and may express a question, statement, command, or exclamation. Sentences are usually formed so that they consist of a main clause and sometimes one or multiple subordinate clauses (see *clause*). Sentences begin with a capital letter and end with an end mark. A sentence expresses a complete thought.

Smallest Space Analysis (SSA)

Smallest space analysis (SSA), which has also been called similarity structure analysis (see Amar and Levy, 2014; Borg and Lingoes, 1987), is a multi-dimensional scaling form of statistical analysis. Both of the names for the procedure are illustrative of its function, as the procedure attempts to discover configuration between and of variables in a research project which are inter-correlated. SSA is based upon the non-metric similarities between variables which it attempts to locate within a theoretical geometric space of the fewest dimensions possible. Thus, smallest space analysis is a data analysis technique similar in some ways to factor analysis but using non-metric rankings of items in its analysis rather than raw data as used in other techniques. The use of non-metric measures creates the potential for the use of smallest space analysis in a more flexible manner upon data that is less stringent in terms of its statistical requirements and also open qualitative, theoretical, or philosophical judgements and estimations of similarity. The output of SSA is a series of two-dimensional plots, the accuracy of which is estimated through a co-efficient of alienation.

Test Battery

In psychological assessment, individuals are usually tested using a variety of different, though related, tests. This is the case in the assessment of intelligence and other skills and abilities. Together, these tests are known as a test battery.

Theory

The word *theory* has slightly different meanings, but in this book, a theory is taken to be related to a set of ideas which are used to explain other events or things. Theories are often general in their nature and are independent of the events, states of affairs, and so on, that they are being employed to explain. In science, theories are often used in this sense in order to explain the natural world in a manner that avails itself to investigation and verification, refutation or amendment through the process of repeated investigation of the theory's ability to provide explanations of empirical observations.

Traditional Mapping Sentence

(See *mapping sentence [in a general sense]*).

Truthmaker

The notion of a *truthmaker* originates and resides within metaphysical philosophy and is encompassed within concerns regarding truth and existence. Thus, the thing that confers truthbearer truth is its truthmaker. In an elemental sense, this implies that this relationship "holds between any truthmaker, T, which is something in the world, and the proposition" that T exists (Armstrong, 2004, p. 6).

Validity

Validity refers to the instance when something is rooted in truth or fact, supported by a law, and so on. Perhaps of more direct relevance to the present writing, validity means something that is supported by theoretical rationale or empirical evidence. Moreover, validity implicates an adequacy and appropriateness in terms of any conclusions that are derived from research or other forms of assessment (American Psychological Association, 2018).

Variables

Variables are components of experimental situations and a part of the language used to talk about and describe much quantitative research. Variables are events or other entities that may be controlled, altered, or measured in an experiment. More specifically, in experiments, variables may take one of several types. Independent variables are the variables that are manipulated in the course of an experiment. Dependent variables are the outcome variables or the variables that alter because of the manipulation of the independent variables. Controlled variables are the variables that are held constant in an experiment in order to remove their effects upon the dependent variables. Extraneous variables are the variables that have an effect upon the dependent variables but are not taken into account when considering the effects of the independent variables. Extraneous variables are a source of error in an experiment.

Notes

1. The same or broadly similar glossary appeared in Hackett (2020).
2. In original research within facet theory, the range facet is always present and specified prior to data collection.

References

Amar, R., and Levy, S. (2014) SSA: Similarity Structure Analysis, in Michalos, A.C. (ed.) *Encyclopedia of Quality of Life and Well-Being Research*, New York: Springer, 6306–6313.

American Psychological Association. (2018) *APA Dictionary of Psychology*. Retrieved from https://dictionary.apa.org/cognition.

Armstrong, D.M. (2004) *Truth and Truth-makers*, Cambridge: Cambridge University Press.

Borg, I., and Lingoes, J. (1987) *Multidimensional Similarity Structure Analysis*, New York: Springer.

Borg, I., and Mohler, P.P. (2011) *Trends and Perspectives in Empirical Social Research*, Berlin: Walter de Gruyter.

Brown, J.M. (1985) An Introduction to the Uses of Facet Theory, in Canter, D. (ed.) *Facet Theory: Approaches to Social Research*, New York: Springer Verlag.

Brown, J.M. (2010) Designing Research Using Facet Theory, in Brown, J.M., and Campbell, E.A. (eds.) *The Cambridge Handbook of Forensic Psychology*, Cambridge: Cambridge University Press, 795–802.

Canter, D. (ed.) (1985) *Facet Theory: Approaches to Social Research*, New York: Springer Verlag.

Coxon, A.P.M. (1982) *The User's Guide to Multi-Dimensional Scaling with Special Reference to the MDS (X) Library of Computer Programs*, London: Heinemann Educational.

Elizur, D., and Shye, S. (1976) The Inclination to Reimmigrate: A Structural Analysis of the Case of Israelis Residing in France and in the USA, *Human Relations*, 29, 73–84.

Gabriel, R.K. (1954) Simplex Structure of the Progressive Matrices Test, *British Journal of Statistical Psychology*, 7(1), 9–14.

Guttman, L. (1944) A Basis for Scaling Quantitative Data, *American Sociological Review*, 9(2), 139–150.

Hackett, P.M.W. (1995) *Conservation and the Consumer: Understanding Environmental Concern*, London: Routledge.

Hackett, P.M.W. (2014) *Facet Theory and the Mapping Sentence: Evolving Philosophy, Use and Application*, Basingstoke: Palgrave McMillan Publishers.

Hackett, P.M.W. (2016a) *Psychology and Philosophy of Abstract Art: Neuroaesthetics, Perception and Comprehension*, Basingstoke: Palgrave.

Hackett, P.M.W. (2016b) *The Perceptual Structure of Three-Dimensional Art*, Heidelberg: Springer.

Hackett, P.M.W. (2016c) Facet Theory and the Mapping Sentence as Hermeneutically Consistent Structured Meta-Ontology and Structured Meta-Mereology, *Frontiers in Psychology: Philosophical and Theoretical Psychology*, 7, 471. https://doi.org/10.3389/fpsyg.2016.00471.

Hackett, P.M.W. (2018) Declarative Mapping Sentence Mereologies: Categories From Aristotle to Lowe, in Hackett, P.M.W. (ed.) *Mereologies, Ontologies and Facets: The Categorial Structure of Reality*, Lanham, MD: Lexington Publishers.

Hackett, P.M.W. (2020) *The Complexity of Bird Behaviour: A Facet Theory Approach*, Cham, CH: Springer.

Hawley, K. (2017) Social Mereology, *Journal of the American Philosophical Association*, 3(4), 395–411.

Hildebrandt, L. (1986) A Facet Theoretical Approach for Testing Measurement and Structural Theories: An Application of Confirmatory Mds, in Lutz, R.J. (ed.) *Advances in Consumer Research Volume 13*, Provo, UT: Association for Consumer Research, 523–528.

Lawrence, J., and Noonan, B. (2018) Avian Learning Favors Colors, not Bright, Signals, *PLoS One*, 13(3), e0194279.

Leśniewski, S. (1927–1931) O podstawach matematyki, *Przegląd Filozoficzny*, 30, 164–206; 31, 261–291; 32, 60–101; 33, 77–105; 34, 142–170; Eng. trans. by D. I. Barnett: 'On the Foundations of Mathematics', in S. Leśniewski, *Collected Works* (ed. by S. J. Surma et al.), Dordrecht: Kluwer, 1992, Vol. 1, pp. 174–382.

Lingoes, J.C., and Borg, I. (1977) Identifying Spatial Manifolds for Interpretation, in Lingoes, J.C. (ed.) *Geometric Representations of Relational Data*, Ann Arbor: Mathesis Press.

Mennill, D.J., Doucet, S.M., Newman, A.E.M., Williams, H., Moran, I.G., Thomas, I.P., Woodworth, B.K., and Norris, D.R. (2018) Wild Birds Learn Songs from

Experimental Vocal Tutors, *Current Biology*, 28(20), 3273–3278. https://doi.org/10.1016/j.cub.2018.08.011.

Petranovich, S. (2018) Husserlian Mereology and Intimate Community Membership, *The Journal of Speculative Philosophy*, 32(3), 462–474.

Pietruszczak, A. (2018) *Metamereology* (revised and extended English version), translated by Matthew Carmody, Gagarina, Poland: The Nicolaus Copernicus University Scientific Publishing House.

Raveh, A., and Landau, S.F. (1993) Partial Order Scalogram Analysis with Base Coordinates (POSAC): Its Application to Crime Patterns in All the States in the United States, *Journal of Quantitative Criminology*, 9(1), 83–99.

Ruben, D.-H. (1983) Social Wholes and Parts, *Mind*, 92, 219–238.

Runkel, P.J., and McGrath, J.E. (1972) *Research on Human Behaviour: A Systematic Guide to Method*, New York: Hold Rinehart and Winston.

Strohmaier, D. (2019) Group Membership and Parthood, *Journal of Social Ontology*, 4(2), 121–135.

Thomasson, A. (2018) Categories, in Zalta, E.N. (ed.) *The Stanford Encyclopedia of Philosophy* (Spring 2018 ed.). Retrieved from https://plato.stanford.edu/archives/spr2018/entries/categories/.

Varzi, A. (2016) *Mereology: The Stanford Encyclopedia of Philosophy* (Winter 2016 ed.), E.N. Zalta (ed.). Retrieved from https://plato.stanford.edu/archives/win2016/entries/mereology/.

Index

Note: Numbers in *italics* indicate a figure. Numbers in **bold** indicate a table.